THE MOSTLY VEGETABLE MENU COOKBOOK

THE MOSTLY VEGETABLE

MENU COOKBOOK

NANCY B. KATZ

GROSSET & DUNLAP   PUBLISHERS • NEW YORK

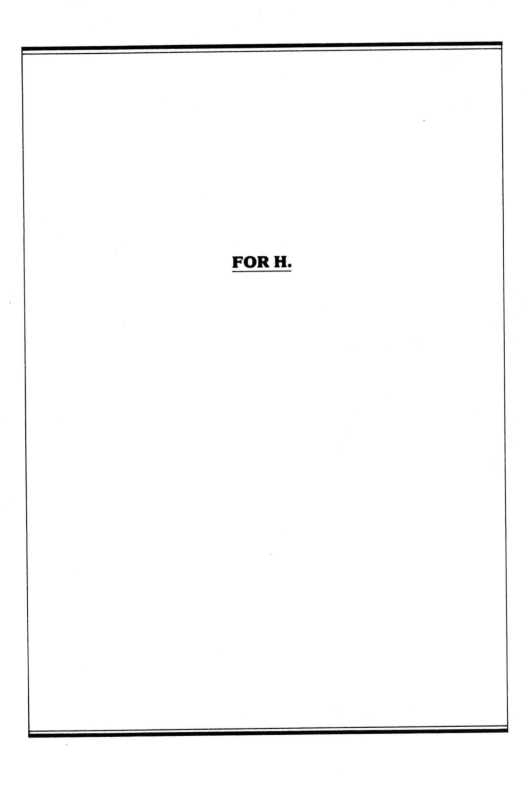

FOR H.

C O N T E N T S

INTRODUCTION

The idea for this book began to develop about a year ago, after a really dreadful vegetarian dinner at the home of an acquaintance. The main course consisted of a vegetarian meatloaf. This positively unappetizing dish was accompanied by zucchini cooked in orange juice—no oil or butter because our hosts were watching their cholesterol intake. I am sure there was a first course, which I've thankfully forgotten.

I have written this book to illustrate that it is possible to create exciting and sophisticated menus based mostly on vegetables. I am not a vegetarian, and this is not a book for vegetarians. These meals are for people who, like me, love to cook, people who will enjoy serving a mostly vegetarian meal that is long on style. I do not believe it is necessary to meditate over the "mystique" of tofu (just enjoy it!) or have a cosmic experience with bean sprouts and yogurt. You will not find recipes that try to simulate a meat flavor or texture by using soybeans or ground nuts. And you won't have to do all your marketing at the local health food store.

It will come as no surprise to anyone who cooks (or eats) that fresh vegetables are delicious and wholesome. And let's face it—vegetables are the answer to how you can feed your family economically. With very few exceptions, all the recipes are based on fresh vegetables in season. In the case of the tomato, which has a short season, you can often substitute the canned product and obtain good results. For the sake of convenience and flavor I have used beef stock or chicken stock in the preparation of soups. You will also find a few appetizers that are not strictly vegetarian.

Many people who are good cooks and who are able to follow recipes accurately have difficulty assembling a menu in which all the parts complement one another. This problem is compounded in vegetable cookery where the use of meat, fish, and poultry has been eliminated. For this reason I have organized the recipes around menus. And of course you can reorganize the menus to suit your taste and needs.

Friends have often commented that this cuisine is time-consuming. I won't deny that many of the dishes do take time to make. Happily, however, many of the chopping, slicing, and pureeing tasks are quickly and easily accomplished with the aid of a food processor or blender. Every menu has at least one recipe that can be made in stages or ahead of time. Often the first course and dessert are prepared the day before. Soups in most cases may be readied in advance and reheated just before serving. Throughout, there are suggestions about organizing your preparation time to avoid last-minute frenzy in the kitchen.

I cannot stress enough the importance of using top-quality ingredients. If possible, purchase fruit and vegetables from a greengrocer rather than at the supermarket—you'll find the best selection and you'll get superior produce for your money.

I offer this book as an invitation to expand your menu repertoire. The basic commitment here is to increasing your pleasure in food.

Nancy B. Katz

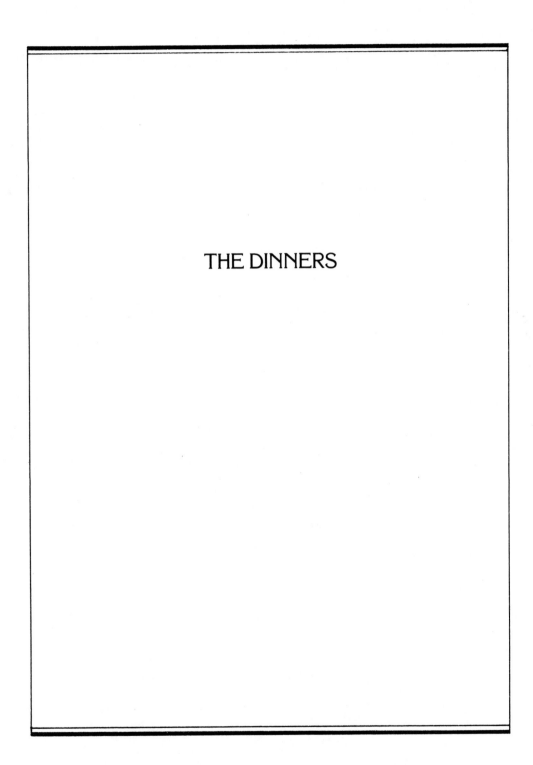

THE DINNERS

| D | I | N | N | E | R | | 1 |

TOMATO MULLIGATAWNY SOUP

BOMBAY VEGETABLE CURRY

CURRANT RICE

CUCUMBER-YOGURT SALAD

COLD LEMON SOUFFLÉ

One of the more pleasant aspects of this dinner is the delightful aroma that fills the kitchen while you are preparing the mulligatawny soup and the vegetable curry. The soup, salad, and dessert can all be prepared well in advance; the rice, of course, should be made as close to serving time as possible, but if tightly covered, it will remain fluffy and warm for up to 15 minutes. The vegetables in the curry should be crisp-tender, so plan to serve it soon after it is ready.

Tomato Mulligatawny Soup   SERVES 4

Now, thanks to the blender and food processor, perfectly pureed soups of velvety texture are within the capabilities of everyone. This is one such soup —it is lightly thickened with a puree of its own vegetables and mildly spiced with curry, hot red pepper, and cumin.

13

3	Tbs. butter	1½	Tbs. curry powder
1	large onion, coarsely chopped	½	tsp. dried cumin
2	stalks celery, coarsely chopped	⅛	tsp. dried hot red pepper flakes
1	large carrot, coarsely chopped	4½	cups chicken stock (p. 207) or 2½ cups canned chicken broth and 2 cups water
4	medium tomatoes, peeled, seeded, and chopped, or 2 cups canned tomatoes, drained	1	Tbs. fresh chopped coriander leaves (Chinese parsley)

1. Melt the butter in a large heavy saucepan. Add the onion, celery, and carrot; sauté until soft. Stir in the tomatoes and cook, uncovered, over medium heat for 5 minutes.

2. Sprinkle the curry powder, cumin, and dried pepper flakes over the vegetables. Cook, stirring over low heat for several minutes.

3. Pour in the chicken stock, bring to a boil. Reduce the heat and simmer, covered, for 30 minutes.

4. Remove the solids from the soup and puree them in a blender or food processor. Return the puree to the liquid and heat through. Garnish each serving with chopped coriander.

Bombay Vegetable Curry   SERVES 4

Here is a very good vegetable curry in which all the vegetables retain their texture and character. This is not, as I have often experienced, an overcooked blend of vegetables that becomes unrecognizable. For this dish each component is cooked separately, then all are brought together and simmered briefly with aromatic spices.

1	medium eggplant (about	⅛	tsp. cayenne pepper (or
	1¼ pounds)		more, according to taste)
	Salt	¼	tsp. ground cumin
¼	cup vegetable oil	1	large clove garlic, minced
1	large carrot, sliced thin	2	medium tomatoes peeled,
1	large green or red bell		seeded, and chopped (about
	pepper, sliced thin		1 cup), or 1 cup canned
1	cup sliced onions		tomatoes, drained
1	Tbs. curry powder		

1. Peel the eggplant and cut it into 1-inch cubes. Sprinkle with salt and place the eggplant in a colander with a weight on it (a heavy cast iron pot will do). Let it drain this way for 40 minutes. Dry well between pieces of paper toweling.

2. Heat the oil in a large heavy skillet; when it is quite hot, add the carrot and pepper and stir-fry for one minute. Remove to a bowl with a slotted spoon. To the same skillet add the eggplant and sauté until tender and browned. Add the cooked eggplant to the reserved carrot and pepper mixture.

3. If necessary, add 1 tablespoon more of oil to the skillet and sauté the sliced onions until they are golden. Add the curry powder, cayenne pepper, cumin, and minced garlic and cook over low heat, stirring for 2 minutes. Stir in the tomatoes, cover the pan, and simmer for 5 minutes. Add the reserved eggplant mixture, combine well, and simmer the curry, covered, for 10 minutes. Serve hot with currant rice.

Currant Rice   SERVES 4

2	Tbs. butter	¼	tsp. ground allspice
1	cup white rice	½	cup canned chicken broth
2	Tbs. dried currants	1	cup water
½	bay leaf		

1. Heat the butter in a heavy saucepan. Add the rice and cook until it just begins to color. Add the currants, bay leaf, and allspice. Stir and cook another minute or two.

2. Add the liquids, bring to a boil. Reduce the heat and simmer, covered for 18 minutes or until all the liquid has been absorbed by the rice. Serve hot.

Cucumber-Yogurt Salad   SERVES 4

3 medium-sized cucumbers, peeled, seeded, and sliced thin Salt 1 Tbs. olive oil	¼ tsp. ground cumin 1 clove garlic, crushed 1 Tbs. grated onion 1 cup plain yogurt

1. Salt the cucumber slices and let them drain in a colander for 35 minutes. Rinse briefly under cold running water and pat dry with paper toweling.

2. Place the cucumbers in a mixing bowl. Stir in the olive oil, add the remaining ingredients, and combine well. Refrigerate for at least one hour.

Cold Lemon Soufflé   SERVES 4–6

This is a splendid-looking make-ahead dessert that always elicits praise.

1 Tbs. unflavored gelatin (one package) ½ cup lemon juice 1½ cups milk 4 egg yolks ½ cup sugar	Grated rind of 2 lemons ½ cup heavy cream 4 egg whites, stiffly beaten 4 amaretti (Italian macaroons), crushed

1. Sprinkle the gelatin over the lemon juice to soften for about 10 minutes.

2. Bring the milk to a gentle boil in the top of a double boiler over direct heat.

3. In a large mixing bowl beat the egg yolks and sugar together until the mixture is pale yellow and forms a ribbon. Pour the boiling milk over the yolks, stirring constantly; return it to the double boiler and place over simmering water. Continue to stir until the mixture thickens and coats a spoon. Remove from the heat. Stir in the softened gelatin and lemon rind.

4. Turn the warm custard into a large mixing bowl and refrigerate until thickened (do not let gel completely).

5. Whip the cream until it holds soft peaks. Gently fold the cream into the custard. Fold in the stiffly beaten egg whites and turn the mixture into a 1-quart soufflé case fitted with a 3-inch collar of oiled foil. Chill for at least 3 hours or overnight. Remove the collar and dust the top of the soufflé with crushed amaretti.

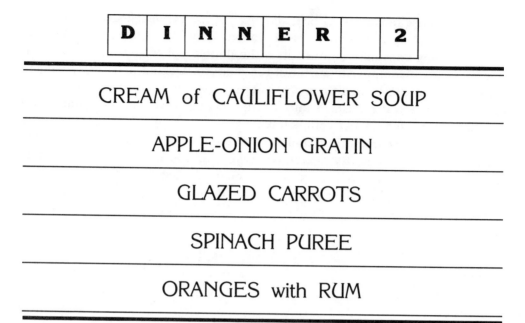

DINNER 2

CREAM of CAULIFLOWER SOUP

APPLE-ONION GRATIN

GLAZED CARROTS

SPINACH PUREE

ORANGES with RUM

Here is a menu to brighten the grayest of winter days.

Cream of Cauliflower Soup   SERVES 4

If you think you don't like cauliflower, you'll certainly change your mind after you've tasted this soothing soup. It's full of flavor and body; serve it well chilled in the summertime and everyone will swear it's vichyssoise!

3   Tbs. butter
1   medium onion, chopped
1   large clove garlic, chopped
1   cauliflower, about 2 pounds
    cut into flowerets

5   cups chicken stock (p. 207)
    or 3 cups canned chicken
    broth and 2 cups water
¼   cup light cream
⅛   tsp. freshly ground black
    pepper
    Pinch of cayenne pepper

1. Heat the butter in a large heavy kettle. Add the onion and garlic. Cook over low heat until soft.

2. Add the cauliflower and chicken stock. Bring to a boil. Reduce the heat and simmer, covered, for about 40 minutes or until the cauliflower is very soft.

3. Remove the solids from the soup and puree in a blender or food processor. Return the puree to the liquid and stir in the cream and seasonings. Heat through without boiling. Serve hot. To serve cold, refrigerate overnight and garnish each serving with chopped chives.

Apple-Onion Gratin   SERVES 4

Apples and onions may strike you as an odd combination, but it is a classic Normandy mixture that in various forms usually accompanies roast pork. Here it gets star billing, served with a bright green spinach purée and tender glazed carrots. An excellent and colorful choice for a winter dinner.

1½	pounds onions, coarsely sliced	⅓	cup heavy cream
2	pounds tart apples, peeled, cored, sliced thin	6	Tbs. melted butter
		1	Tbs. lemon juice
2	Tbs. brown sugar	1	cup fresh bread crumbs

PREHEAT THE OVEN TO 350°.

1. Combine all the ingredients except the bread crumbs in a large mixing bowl.

2. Turn the mixture into a well-buttered 3-quart casserole or baking dish. Bake in a preheated 350° oven for 1 hour, sprinkle with bread crumbs, and bake another 50 minutes or until the apples are quite soft and the crumbs lightly browned. May be kept warm in the turned-off oven for 20 minutes.

Glazed Carrots   SERVES 4

1	pound finger carrots, scraped, left whole		Salt and pepper to taste
3	Tbs. butter	1	cup water
1	Tbs. sugar	1	Tbs. chopped parsley

Put the carrots, butter, sugar, salt and pepper, and water in a small saucepan. Bring to a boil. Cover, reduce the heat, and simmer for 30 minutes or until the carrots are tender and the liquid has reduced to a glaze. Serve hot, sprinkled with chopped parsley.

Spinach Puree   SERVES 4

2	pounds fresh spinach, tough stems removed		Pinch of nutmeg
3	Tbs. butter		Salt and pepper
2	Tbs. chopped shallots	2	Tbs. heavy cream (optional)

1. Rinse the spinach and plunge it into a large kettle of boiling water. Cook, covered, just until the spinach has wilted. Remove and drain immediately. Wring in a kitchen towel to extract excess moisture. Puree the spinach in a food processor or blender.

2. Heat the butter in a large enameled saucepan. Add the shallots and cook until soft. Stir in the spinach and cook over medium heat until heated through. Add nutmeg, salt, and pepper to taste. Stir in the heavy cream if desired. The spinach may be kept warm in a pan over simmering water.

Oranges with Rum   SERVES 4

3	large navel oranges	2	Tbs. dark rum
1	Tbs. sugar		Fresh mint

1. Peel the oranges and remove the white pith. Cut into ¼-inch-thick slices.

2. Place the slices in a serving dish. Sprinkle with sugar and rum. Cover and macerate in the refrigerator for 2 hours. Serve chilled. Garnish each serving with a sprig of fresh mint.

D I N N E R 3

ASPARAGUS MILANESE

LINGUINE with FOUR CHEESES

MARINATED MIXED SALAD

PEAR TART FRANGIPANE

Asparagus Milanese   SERVES 4

Vegetables that are prepared *alla milanese,* Milan style, are usually dipped in beaten egg and then rolled in fine dry bread crumbs and gently fried. This is a particularly good way to cook asparagus—their sweet flavor emerges lightly wrapped in a crisp coating. Be sure to choose fresh, young, unblemished asparagus with tightly closed tips.

24	fresh, thin asparagus, peeled	⅓	cup freshly grated Parmesan cheese
1	egg		
½	cup dry unflavored bread crumbs	½	cup vegetable oil
			Salt

1. Trim the bottom of each asparagus, leaving a stalk about 5 inches long.
2. Beat the egg lightly in a large flat soup plate.
3. Combine the bread crumbs and cheese; spread on a large plate. Dip the asparagus in the egg, then gently roll it in the crumbs, coating each stalk well. (May be prepared an hour ahead to this point and refrigerated.)
4. Heat the oil in a large heavy skillet over high heat. Fry the asparagus

21

in batches until lightly crisp and golden, a matter of minutes. Remove from the pan and drain on paper toweling. Add salt to taste and serve immediately.

Linguine with Four Cheeses   SERVES 4

These days, everyone must be aware of the virtues of pasta, not the least of which are its reasonable cost and its great variety. Homemade pasta is indeed a treat, and if you have the time and the space, do try it. There are a number of good books on the subject of pasta making, so I will not go into it here. Any of the excellent imported commercial brands also give good results. Ignore the cooking times indicated on the package—they are invariably wrong. The best way to test for the doneness of pasta is to taste it from time to time as it cooks. It must be firm to the bite—the Italians say *al dente.* Overcooked pasta simply does not taste very good! And please, serve it as soon as it is sauced; cold pasta does not taste very good either.

The recipe that follows, linguine with four cheeses, is from the Emilia-Romagna region of Italy. You can prepare the cheese sauce in the time it takes for the water to boil for the pasta. Keep it warm over very low heat until the linguine is ready.

½   **cup butter, softened**
¼   **pound gorgonzola cheese, crumbled**
¼   **pound fresh mozzarella cheese, diced**
¼   **pound fontina cheese, diced**

1   **pound linguine**
½   **cup freshly grated Parmesan cheese**
    Freshly ground black pepper

1. In a heavy saucepan large enough to accommodate the cooked pasta, melt the butter over low heat. Add the gorgonzola, mozzarella, and fontina. Stir constantly until the cheeses have melted. Keep warm over very low heat (use a "flame tamer").

2. Cook the linguine in 6 quarts of rapidly boiling water until it is *al dente* (firm to the bite; do not overcook). Drain the pasta well, add to the saucepan with the cheese sauce and toss to coat. Stir in the Parmesan cheese. Add freshly ground black pepper to taste. Serve immediately on warmed plates.

Marinated Mixed Salad   SERVES 4

This salad should be dressed and refrigerated for about 1½ hours; the flavor improves as it marinates.

¾	pound fresh string beans	2	Tbs. lemon juice
½	medium red onion, sliced thin	4	Tbs. vegetable oil
1	large green bell pepper, cut in julienne strips	4	Tbs. olive oil
4	radishes, sliced thin	½	tsp. minced garlic
3	stalks celery, diced		Salt
1	Tbs. minced parsley		Freshly ground black pepper
¼	tsp. dried oregano		Lettuce leaves

1. Trim the beans; if long, cut them in half. Drop into rapidly boiling water, cover, and cook 40 seconds. Drain immediately under cold running water. Pat dry with paper toweling. Refrigerate until cool.

2. In a large mixing bowl combine the beans with the remaining cut vegetables; sprinkle with parsley and oregano.

3. Whisk together the lemon juice, vegetable oil, olive oil, and garlic. Add salt and freshly ground black pepper to taste. Pour the dressing over the salad and refrigerate for about 1½ hours. Serve on plates lined with lettuce leaves.

Pear Tart Frangipane   SERVES 4–6

I don't usually advocate the use of canned fruit, but here I make an exception. After this tart is baked and glazed, it is very difficult for anyone to tell that it has been prepared with canned pears. You may, of course, make it with fresh pears if you're in the mood to peel and poach them. But why not make things a little easier? You may assemble and refrigerate the tart many hours before you actually plan to bake it.

1	recipe pâte brisée sucrée (p. 203)	1	cup finely ground blanched almonds
4	oz. butter, softened	1	29-oz. can pear halves, drained
½	cup sugar		Apricot glaze (p. 206)
2	eggs, at room temperature		

1. Roll the dough out to a thickness of ⅛ inch. Fit it into a 9-inch tart pan with removable ring. Let rest in the refrigerator for at least 2 hours.

2. Prepare the frangipane (almond cream). Cream the butter and sugar in the bowl of an electric mixer. Add the eggs one at a time, mix well, and add the ground almonds. Combine the mixture well. Refrigerate if not used immediately.

PREHEAT THE OVEN TO 425°.

3. Prick the bottom of the tart shell all over with a fork. Spread the frangipane evenly over the bottom of the shell; arrange the pear halves cut side down over it. Bake in a preheated 425° oven for 50 to 60 minutes (cover the tart with foil if the frangipane browns too quickly). Remove from the oven and brush with apricot glaze. Serve warm or at room temperature.

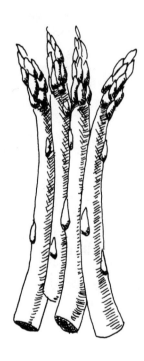

TOFU with SOY DRESSING

HOT-and-SPICY BRAISED EGGPLANT

STIR-FRIED SPINACH

FRESH PINEAPPLE with MINT

Here is an oriental-inspired menu that is always a hit. To bring this menu off smoothly, be sure to have in front of you all the ingredients you'll need. Cooking time here is very brief, so it is important to have everything ready and at your fingertips.

Tofu with Soy Dressing   SERVES 4

Tofu (bean curd) is becoming increasingly popular in this country. It is an excellent and inexpensive source of protein; it is low in calories and tastes delicious. Fresh tofu is always available at oriental grocers; recently many supermarkets have begun to carry it. In the recipe that follows, the tofu takes only minutes to heat through, so prepare the dressing first and set it aside. Oriental sesame oil, with its distinctive aroma and flavor, is essential for the dressing.

FOR THE SOY DRESSING:

2½	Tbs. soy sauce	½	scallion chopped fine
1½	tsp. rice wine vinegar or red wine vinegar	½	clove garlic, crushed
1	Tbs. oriental sesame oil		Pinch of dried hot red pepper flakes

FOR THE TOFU:

4	cakes fresh tofu (bean curd)		Boiling water

1. In a small bowl whisk together the soy sauce, vinegar, and sesame oil. Stir in the remaining ingredients. Set aside.
2. Drop the tofu into rapidly boiling water to cover. Simmer gently, covered, for 3 to 4 minutes. Remove and drain on paper towels.
3. Cut the tofu into ½-inch-thick slices and arrange on a plate. Pour on the dressing and serve immediately.

Hot-and-Spicy Braised Eggplant   SERVES 4

Hot chili sauce with garlic is what gives this dish its fiery spicy flavor. The sauce is sold in small cans or jars and is available at oriental markets.

2	medium eggplants, about 1–1½ pounds each	2	Tbs. hot chili sauce with garlic
	Salt	1	Tbs. soy sauce
8	dried Chinese black mushrooms	2	Tbs. dry sherry
2	medium red bell peppers	1	Tbs. red wine vinegar
		½	tsp. sugar
		½	cup vegetable oil

1. Cut the eggplant into 2-inch cubes; do not peel. Sprinkle with salt and place in a colander, weighted (a heavy pot will do). Let it drain this way for 30 minutes, then pat dry with toweling.
2. Pour boiling water over the mushrooms and let them soak for 30 minutes. Squeeze between paper towels to remove moisture. Cut off the tough stems, and if the mushrooms are large, cut in half. Set aside.

3. Cut the peppers in half; remove the seeds and white membranes. Cut into 2-inch squares. Set aside.

4. In a small bowl mix together the chili sauce, soy sauce, sherry, vinegar, and sugar. Set aside.

5. Heat the oil in a wok or large skillet. When the oil is hot, sauté the eggplant cubes in batches until lightly browned. Remove with a slotted spoon and drain on paper towels.

6. Discard all but 3 tablespoons of oil in the wok and add the mushrooms and peppers. Cook over high heat, stirring, for about 1 minute. Return the eggplant to the wok. Add the chili sauce mixture, lower the heat and cook, stirring, just until heated through. Serve hot or warm. If desired, serve with plain boiled rice.

Stir-fried Spinach   SERVES 4

1½	pounds fresh spinach		Pinch of sugar
3	Tbs. vegetable oil	2	Tbs. soy sauce
½	cup sliced bamboo shoots		

1. Cut the spinach, including the stems, into manageable pieces. Wash well and shake off excess water. Do not pat dry.

2. Heat the oil in a wok or large skillet over medium-high heat. Add the bamboo shoots; cook, stirring, over high heat for 1 minute.

3. Add the spinach, stirring. Add the sugar and soy sauce. Lower the heat, cover, and simmer 2 minutes. Remove to a serving bowl using a slotted spoon.

Fresh Pineapple with Mint   SERVES 4

A good way to test for ripeness in a pineapple is to pull one of the leaves off the top. If it comes out easily, the pineapple is ripe.

1	fresh ripe pineapple	1	Tbs. fresh chopped mint leaves

1. Cut the top off the pineapple and discard. Cut the pineapple into quarters lengthwise. Cut each quarter into slices about ½ inch thick. Cut away the tough outer skin on each slice.

2. Arrange the slices on a platter and sprinkle with chopped mint leaves.

DINNER 5

CHEDDAR CHEESE SOUP

CRÊPES PIPÉRADE

CELERY SALAD

BAKED PEARS

The best approach to this menu is to start with dessert and work backwards. Everything but the soup may be prepared hours ahead of serving time. If you like, prepare the cooked celery salad the day before.

Cheddar Cheese Soup   SERVES 4

The success of this soup depends upon the cheese. Be sure to use a flavorful, well-aged cheddar. A cheese that is too "young" will curdle when heated. Since this is a very rich soup, I recommend small (cup) servings.

3	Tbs. butter	2	cups diced, aged cheddar, about ¾ pound
2	Tbs. chopped onion		
1½	Tbs. flour	1	Tbs. dry sherry
1¼	cups milk, warmed		Freshly ground black pepper
2¼	cups chicken stock (p. 207) or canned chicken broth		Paprika

29

1. Heat the butter in a large heavy saucepan. Add the onions and cook over medium heat until soft. Sprinkle on the flour and cook, stirring, for 3 minutes. Do not let the flour brown.

2. Add the warm milk and stir over medium heat until slightly thickened. Add the broth. Gradually add the cheese, stirring constantly with a wooden spoon. Do not let the soup boil. When the cheese has melted completely and the soup is very smooth, add the sherry and ground pepper to taste. The soup may be kept warm for about half an hour on an asbestos pad over low heat. Sprinkle with paprika before serving.

Crêpes Pipérade   SERVES 4

Pipérade is a Provençal vegetable mixture that resembles ratatouille. Fresh peppers, onions, tomatoes, garlic, and herbs are all sautéed together to create a savory filling for this crêpe recipe. Pipérade is a good vegetable accompaniment for chops and roasts.

FOR THE CRÊPES:

Using the basic recipe on p. 203, prepare 8 7-inch crêpes. Cover with a damp cloth and set aside.

FOR THE PIPÉRADE:

3	Tbs. olive oil	2	cloves garlic, minced
2	cups sliced onions	2	Tbs. chopped parsley
2	cups sliced red and green bell peppers	½	tsp. dried oregano
3	ripe tomatoes, peeled, seeded, and juiced, or 1½ cups canned tomatoes, drained		Butter
		¼	cup freshly grated Parmesan cheese

1. Heat the oil in a large heavy skillet. Add the onions and cook until tender. Add the peppers and cook another 3 to 4 minutes. Chop the tomatoes

and add them to the skillet with the garlic. Cover and cook until the tomatoes give off their liquid. Uncover, raise the heat, and cook until the liquid almost evaporates. Season with the herbs. May be prepared ahead to this point and kept at room temperature.

PREHEAT THE OVEN TO 400°.

2. Place about 2 tablespoons of the pipérade on each crêpe. Roll them and arrange seam side down in a buttered oven-proof dish. Dot with butter and sprinkle with Parmesan cheese. Bake in a preheated 400° oven for 15 minutes.

Celery Salad   SERVES 4

½	bunch celery, sliced	1	Tbs. red wine vinegar
2	cups chicken stock (p. 207)	¼	cup olive oil
	or 1 cup canned chicken		Freshly ground black pepper
	broth and 1 cup water	1	Tbs. chopped parsley

1. Put the celery and stock in a medium saucepan. Cook, uncovered, over high heat for 10 minutes. The celery should remain crisp-tender; do not overcook.

2. Drain the celery (save the broth for use in soups) and refrigerate.

3. Just before serving, whisk together the vinegar and olive oil. Add freshly ground black pepper to taste. Pour the dressing over the celery, toss well, and garnish with chopped parsley.

Baked Pears   SERVES 4

As the pears bake in a wine-flavored syrup, their skins become lightly browned. If desired, serve the pears with sweetened whipped cream for a beautiful dessert presentation.

3	cups water		1	piece stick cinnamon
1	cup white wine		4	firm ripe pears, Anjou or
¾	cup sugar			Bartlett
4	whole cloves			

PREHEAT THE OVEN TO 325°.

1. In a saucepan combine the water, wine, and sugar with the cloves and cinnamon. Bring to a boil. Reduce the heat and simmer, covered, for 20 minutes.

2. Cut a slice from the bottom of each pear—they must stand upright during the baking. Choose a soufflé case or small casserole that will just hold the pears. Pour the heated syrup over the pears to cover them by half. Bake, uncovered, in a preheated 325° oven for 40 minutes. Remove from the oven and allow the pears to cool in the syrup. Serve at room temperature.

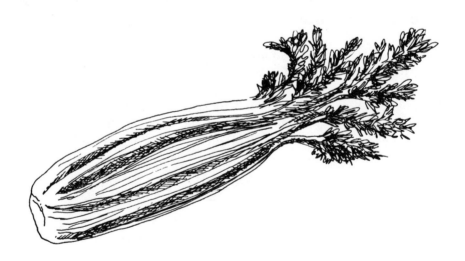

| **D** | **I** | **N** | **N** | **E** | **R** | | **6** |

HOT BORSCHT with YOGURT and DILL

CABBAGE STRUDEL

BULGUR PILAF

APRICOTS in COGNAC

This menu is a cabbage lover's delight! The beet and cabbage borscht is a hearty and warming first course well suited to a cold winter's day. The cabbage strudel, which is 100 percent Hungarian and 100 percent delicious, is one of my favorites.

Hot Borscht with Yogurt and Dill   SERVES 6

3	Tbs. vegetable oil	1	cup canned tomatoes, drained and chopped
1	large onion, chopped		
3	cups coarsely shredded cabbage	1/3	cup red wine vinegar
		6	cups beef stock (p. 208) or 3 cups canned beef broth and 3 cups water
1	clove garlic, crushed		
4	medium beets, peeled and cut in julienne strips or shredded		Yogurt
			Fresh chopped dill

33

1. Heat the oil in a large heavy kettle. Add the onion and sauté until wilted. Add the cabbage and garlic; cook over low heat, stirring occasionally, until the cabbage wilts.

2. Add the remaining ingredients. Bring to a boil, reduce the heat, and simmer, partially covered, until the beets are tender, about 1 hour. Serve the soup with a dollop of yogurt and garnish each serving with fresh chopped dill.

Cabbage Strudel   SERVES 6

Strudel dough is available in specialty food shops and some supermarkets. Be sure the package of strudel leaves has been at room temperature for three hours before proceeding with the recipe. Once you have removed the strudel from its package, keep the sheets you are not working with covered with a damp kitchen towel.

1	head cabbage, about 2 pounds, cored and shredded		Freshly ground black pepper
	Salt	4	strudel leaves
3	Tbs. vegetable oil	4	ounces butter, melted
1	medium onion, chopped	¼	cup fine dry bread crumbs

1. Sprinkle the shredded cabbage liberally with salt and let it stand in a large bowl for 20 minutes. Wring in a large kitchen towel to remove moisture.

2. Heat the vegetable oil in a large heavy skillet or sauté pan. Brown the onion lightly. Add the cabbage and cook until it is wilted and well browned. Stir from time to time to prevent sticking. Sprinkle with pepper to taste. Let cool completely.

PREHEAT THE OVEN TO 350°.

3. Place one strudel leaf on a dampened kitchen towel. Working quickly, brush it with melted butter and sprinkle with 1 tablespoon bread crumbs. Repeat this process with the remaining strudel leaves.

4. Spread the cabbage filling in a thick row down the long end of the dough. Lifting the ends of the towel, carefully and loosely roll up the dough, enfolding the filling completely.

5. Place the strudel roll seam side down on a lightly buttered baking sheet. Brush the top and sides with melted butter. Bake in a preheated 350° oven for 30 minutes or until nicely browned and puffed. Cut the strudel into thick slices and serve hot. Fully baked cabbage strudel may be refrigerated overnight; to reheat, place in a 350° oven for about 20 minutes to heat through.

Bulgur Pilaf   SERVES 6

For a change, instead of rice or noodles, try bulgur (cracked wheat) pilaf. Many supermarkets carry bulgur, but be sure not to buy the packaged, preseasoned variety. Specialty food shops always have bulgur wheat in bulk; look for it in the grains section.

2	Tbs. butter	2	cups chicken stock (p. 207), heated, or 1 cup canned chicken broth and 1 cup water
¼	cup minced shallots, onions, or scallions		
1	cup bulgur (cracked wheat)	3	Tbs. chopped parsley or mint or a mixture of the two

1. Heat the butter in a medium saucepan. Add the shallots and cook until wilted.
2. Stir in the bulgur and sauté over high heat until the grains are coated with butter.
3. Add the heated stock and simmer, covered, for 18 minutes. Stir in the parsley or mint and serve immediately.

Apricots in Cognac   SERVES 6

A very extravagant dessert for deserving friends. The apricots should macerate in the cognac for at least 24 hours, but the longer you leave them (for up to a week), the better they get.

1	pound good quality dried apricots	⅓	cup sugar
			Cognac to cover

Put the apricots in a mixing bowl. Sprinkle with sugar and pour on the cognac. Let stand, covered, at room temperature for at least 24 hours. Chill before serving.

COLD CREAM of SORREL SOUP

NIÇOISE TOMATO TART

THREE-BEAN SALAD

PEACHES in PORT

Cold cream of sorrel soup is an elegant way to begin this pleasant summer dinner for six. Fresh sorrel is widely available from late spring through early fall. Try some in a salad, or cook it (p. 124) and puree it, and serve as an accompaniment to fresh poached salmon.

Cold Cream of Sorrel Soup   SERVES 6

1   pound unblemished sorrel leaves
3   Tbs. butter
¼   cup chopped shallots or onions

3   cups chicken stock (p. 207) or 1½ cups canned chicken broth and 1½ cups water
1   egg yolk
½   cup heavy cream
    Pinch of cayenne pepper

1. Rinse the sorrel and drain well. Remove the stems and cut the leaves into thin shreds. You should have about 5 cups.

2. Heat the butter in a large heavy saucepan. Stir in the shallots and cook until wilted. Add the sorrel and cook, stirring until wilted.

3. Add the broth. Bring to a boil, reduce the heat, and simmer, covered, for about 15 minutes.

4. Remove the solids from the soup and puree them in a blender or food processor. Return the puree to the soup.

5. Whisk together the egg yolk and heavy cream. Slowly dribble and stir the yolk-cream mixture into the soup. Heat through, but do not let the soup boil or it will curdle. Add the cayenne pepper. Serve the soup well chilled; correct the seasonings.

Niçoise Tomato Tart   SERVES 6

Prepare the partially baked pastry shell for this tart early in the day, and the final assembly and baking can be done just before you serve the soup to your guests.

The tart, served with a crisp green salad and a glass of white wine, also makes an excellent lunch.

1 partially baked 9-inch tart shell, cooled (p. 203)	1 Tbs. fresh minced basil or ½ tsp. dried
3 medium-sized ripe tomatoes	⅓ pound fontina cheese, sliced thin
3 Tbs. olive oil	

PREHEAT THE OVEN TO 350°.

1. Cut the tomatoes into ¼-inch-thick slices. Carefully remove the seeds and juice. Place in a shallow plate, pour on the olive oil, and sprinkle with basil. Marinate 15 minutes.

2. Completely cover the bottom of the cooled tart shell with cheese slices. Arrange the tomatoes in an overlapping circular pattern over the cheese. Brush on any remaining marinade. Bake in a preheated 350° oven for 25 minutes. The tart may be kept warm for up to half an hour in the turned-off oven. Serve hot or warm.

Three-Bean Salad   SERVES 6

Here is a salad that uses canned beans to excellent advantage. You can serve this dish any time of the year, since the ingredients are always available.

½   pound fresh string beans
1   cup canned kidney beans, drained
1   cup canned white cannellini beans, drained
1   large red bell pepper, seeded and cubed

½   cup thinly sliced red onion
1   tsp. dried oregano
     Salt and freshly ground black pepper
2   Tbs. red wine vinegar
⅓   cup olive oil

1. Trim the string beans; if long, cut them in half. Drop into rapidly boiling water, cover, and cook 40 seconds. Drain immediately under cold running water. Pat dry with paper toweling. Refrigerate until cool.

2. In a large salad bowl combine the cooled string beans with the canned beans, bell pepper, onion, and oregano. Season with salt and pepper to taste. May be prepared up to 2 hours ahead to this point and refrigerated.

3. Just before serving, whisk together the vinegar and oil. Pour over the salad and toss well.

Peaches in Port   SERVES 6

Fruit macerated in wine or liqueur is a welcome ending to almost any meal. You'll find peaches in port wonderfully refreshing and light, and a breeze to prepare.

6   firm, ripe peaches, peeled
2   Tbs. lemon juice

4   Tbs. superfine sugar (or more, to taste)
2   cups port wine

1. To facilitate peeling, drop the peaches into rapidly boiling water for 20 seconds; you will then be able to slip the skins off easily. Cut the peaches in half, remove the pits, and cut the peaches into ½-inch slices.

2. Place the peaches in a mixing bowl; toss with lemon juice and sugar. Add the port wine to the bowl, cover, and refrigerate for at least 4 hours.

3. Serve the peaches in chilled long-stemmed glasses.

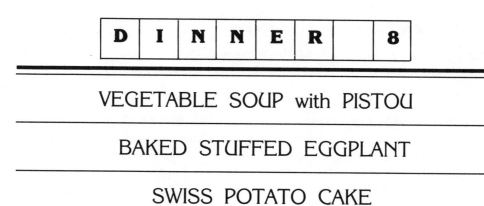

DINNER 8

VEGETABLE SOUP with PISTOU

BAKED STUFFED EGGPLANT

SWISS POTATO CAKE

GINGERED CUSTARD

This is a fairly complicated menu, so I would suggest assembling it in steps, at a leisurely pace, unless you are prepared to work for 3 solid hours! Start by making the dessert either in the morning or the day before you want to serve it; keep refrigerated. Cook and refrigerate the potatoes for the Swiss potato cake several hours before you need them—they should be thoroughly cooled before being grated. The baked stuffed eggplant can be assembled ahead and put into the oven to bake while your guests are having their first course. Try not to prepare the soup too far in advance since the vegetables will become soggy with reheating.

Vegetable Soup with Pistou   SERVES 6

Here is a simplified version of the popular Mediterranean soup known as *soupe au pistou*. The *pistou*, a marvelous "basil paste," is stirred into the soup, giving it its characteristic flavor. For a delicious hors d'oeuvre, try lightly toasted French bread spread with pistou.

Pistou prepared in the blender or food processor is perfectly satisfactory, but making it by hand in a mortar will give it a fuller and more interesting texture; here are recipes for both.

FOR *PISTOU* BY HAND, ABOUT ¾ CUP:

3	large cloves garlic, peeled	5	Tbs. tomato paste
¼	tsp. salt	4	Tbs. olive oil
1	cup fresh basil leaves (packed) or 5 Tbs. dried basil	½	cup freshly grated Parmesan cheese

1. In a mortar pound the garlic with the salt until you have a smooth paste. Mash in the basil.
2. Stir in the tomato paste a tablespoon at a time. Add the olive oil a tablespoon at a time, mixing well after each addition. Gently mix in the grated cheese. *Pistou* keeps well, covered, in the refrigerator for a week. It should be brought to room temperature before using.

FOR *PISTOU* IN A BLENDER OR FOOD PROCESSOR:

Use the same ingredients listed in the preceding recipe. Place all the ingredients except the olive oil in the container of a blender or food processor and process until smooth. With the machine still running, add the olive oil in a slow steady stream.

FOR THE VEGETABLE SOUP:

3	Tbs. olive oil	1	large carrot, sliced thin
1	medium onion, chopped	1	large potato, peeled and cubed
1	large leek, white part only, chopped	½	cup celery leaves, chopped
1	28-oz. can Italian plum tomatoes and their juice	½	pound fresh string beans, cut into 1-inch pieces
⅛	tsp. saffron	½	pound zucchini, cubed
6	cups chicken stock (p. 207) or 3 cups canned chicken broth and 3 cups water		

1. Heat the olive oil in a large heavy kettle. Add the onion and leek and cook, stirring until soft.
2. Drain and chop the tomatoes. Reserve the liquid in which they are

packed. Add the tomatoes and saffron to the kettle; cook over high heat for 3 or 4 minutes. Stir in the stock and tomato liquid; bring to a boil. Add the carrot, potato, and celery leaves. Lower the heat and cook about 10 minutes. Add the string beans and zucchini and cook another 10 to 12 minutes. The vegetables should remain crisp-tender.

3. Put ¼ cup of *pistou* in a mixing bowl; stir in 1 cup of the hot soup and return this to the kettle. Serve the soup hot, passing the remaining *pistou* separately.

Baked Stuffed Eggplant   SERVES 6

3	eggplants (about ½ pound each)
3	Tbs. olive oil
2	cups chopped onion
1	tsp. chopped garlic
1	cup canned tomatoes, drained and chopped
2	Tbs. chopped parsley
½	tsp. dried oregano
¼	pound fresh mozzarella cheese, cubed
4	Tbs. freshly grated Parmesan cheese

PREHEAT THE OVEN TO 375°.

1. Cut the eggplants in half lengthwise. Using a melon ball cutter, scoop out the pulp, leaving a shell about ¼ inch thick. Chop and reserve the pulp. Parboil the shells for 3 minutes; remove immediately and let cool.

2. Heat the oil in a large skillet. Add the onions, garlic, and eggplant pulp. Cook, stirring, until the eggplant pulp is soft, about 8 minutes. Remove to a mixing bowl and add the tomatoes, parsley, oregano, mozzarella, and 2 tablespoons of the Parmesan cheese. Combine the mixture well and fill the reserved eggplant shells with it. May be prepared ahead to this point.

3. Arrange the stuffed eggplant shells in a large baking dish, sprinkle on the remaining 2 tablespoons of Parmesan cheese, and bake in a preheated 375° oven for 35 minutes. Serve hot or warm.

Swiss Potato Cake   SERVES 6

This deservedly famous Swiss potato dish never fails to please. As the outside of the large flat "cake" becomes crisp and brown, the inside remains moist and tender.

2	pounds potatoes	1	Tbs. vegetable oil
4	Tbs. butter		Salt and pepper to taste

    1. Cook the potatoes in their skins in rapidly boiling water for 20 minutes. Peel while still warm. Refrigerate until cool.

    2. Grate the potatoes coarsely. Heat 2 tablespoons of the butter with 1 tablespoon of vegetable oil in a large heavy skillet (cast iron if possible). Add the potatoes and salt and pepper to taste. Using a spatula, press the potatoes into a large flat cake. Add the remaining 2 tablespoons of butter and cook the cake over medium heat until nicely browned. Shake the skillet from time to time to prevent sticking.

    3. Slide the potato cake onto a large flat plate, then return it to the skillet, uncooked side down, and continue cooking until lightly browned and crisp. Serve on an attractive platter and cut the cake into wedges.

Gingered Custard   SERVES 6

Two teaspoons of ground ginger are all it takes to transform a basic custard into a dessert with real interest.

2½	cups milk	3	eggs
½	cup sugar	1	egg yolk
2	tsp. ground ginger	½	tsp. vanilla extract

PREHEAT THE OVEN TO 325°.

    1. Scald the milk with the sugar and ginger.

2. Beat the eggs and yolk lightly. Slowly add the scalded milk, stirring constantly. Add the vanilla.

3. Carefully strain the mixture through a sieve into 6 half-cup custard molds. Place the molds in a pan and add enough boiling water to come halfway up the sides of the molds. Bake in a preheated 325° oven for 1 hour or until a knife inserted down the middle of the custard comes out clean.

4. Serve either at room temperature or chilled, in the molds or unmolded.

| D | I | N | N | E | R | | 9 |

COLD CURRIED ZUCCHINI SOUP

CHUTNEY-STUFFED TOMATOES

INDIAN PILAU

MIXED SALAD with CORIANDER

FRESH RASPBERRY TART

Since I am quite fond of curried dishes, this is one of my favorite menus. I happen to prefer a mild curry powder for flavoring both the curried zucchini soup and the chutney-stuffed tomatoes. You should feel free to experiment with curry powders of varying spiciness. There are some wonderfully hot blends available at Indian grocery stores and shops that specialize in imported foods.

Cold Curried Zucchini Soup   SERVES 6

3 Tbs. butter	1½ Tbs. curry powder
½ cup chopped onions	5 cups chicken stock (p. 207)
1 large clove garlic, chopped	or 3 cups canned chicken
4 medium-sized zucchini	broth and 2 cups water
(about 1½ pounds), sliced	1 cup plain yogurt
thin	

1. Heat the butter in a large heavy saucepan. Add the onion and garlic; cook over low heat until soft.

2. Add the zucchini, raise the heat to medium, and cook, uncovered, for 10 minutes. Stir occasionally.

3. Sprinkle the curry powder over the zucchini. Cook, stirring, for 2 minutes. Add the stock and bring to a boil. Reduce the heat and simmer, covered, for 20 minutes.

4. Remove the solids from the soup and puree them in a blender or food processor. Return the puree to the liquid and refrigerate for 6 hours. Before serving, gradually whisk in the yogurt.

Chutney-stuffed Tomatoes   SERVES 6

6	large, firm, ripe tomatoes	½	tsp. minced garlic
3	Tbs. butter	1½	Tbs. curry powder
1	cup chopped onion	1	bay leaf, crumbled
1	cup chopped celery	3	Tbs. mango chutney

PREHEAT THE OVEN TO 375°.

1. Slice off the top of each tomato. With a melon ball cutter, scoop out the flesh, leaving a shell about ¼ inch thick. Chop and reserve the pulp.

2. Melt the butter in a heavy skillet. Add the onion, celery, and garlic; cook, stirring, until the vegetables wilt. Stir in the curry powder and bay leaf. Add the reserved tomato pulp. Cook over medium heat about 15 minutes. Remove the skillet from the heat and stir in the chutney. Allow the mixture to cool before stuffing the tomatoes.

3. Fill each tomato with the chutney-vegetable mixture. (May be prepared ahead to this point and refrigerated; bring to room temperature before baking.) Arrange the tomatoes in a lightly buttered baking dish. Bake 15 minutes in a preheated 375° oven. Serve hot.

Indian Pilau   SERVES 6

Cardamom is a spice that turns up frequently in Indian cuisine. Here it is combined with cinnamon to produce a fragrant, mildly spiced rice dish that goes well with curried dishes.

3	Tbs. butter	½	cup shelled peas (about ½ pound unshelled)
1¼	cups white rice		
⅛	tsp. cinnamon	2	cups chicken stock (p. 207) or 1 cup canned chicken broth and 1 cup water
¼	tsp. ground cardamom		
3	Tbs. dried currants		

1. Heat the butter in a heavy saucepan. Add the rice and cook until the rice just begins to color. Add the cinnamon and cardamom. Stir and continue cooking another minute or two.

2. Add the remaining ingredients. Bring to a boil. Reduce the heat and simmer, covered, for 20 minutes or until all the liquid is absorbed and the rice is tender. Serve hot or warm.

Mixed Salad with Coriander   SERVES 6

Coriander has a slightly spicy-pungent taste and looks a lot like Italian parsley. Known also as cilantro or Chinese parsley, it can usually be found at the greengrocer. Shops specializing in oriental or Mexican food always have it on hand.

3	medium tomatoes, cubed	2	Tbs. fresh chopped coriander
1	large cucumber, peeled, seeded, and cubed	1½	Tbs. lemon juice
½	cup chopped scallions	4	Tbs. vegetable oil
⅓	cup radishes, sliced thin	⅛	tsp. ground cumin

1. In a large salad bowl combine the tomatoes, cucumber, scallions, radishes, and coriander.

2. Whisk together the lemon juice and vegetable oil. Add the cumin. Pour the dressing over the salad, toss well, and refrigerate for about half an hour before serving.

Fresh Raspberry Tart   SERVES 6

I think raspberries are best when served fresh and unadorned. Here is a very simple but elegant way to serve them in a tart—no pastry cream—just tender, flaky pastry and lightly glazed raspberries.

Currant glaze (p. 206)
1 **fully baked 9-inch sweet tart shell (p. 202), cooled**

1 **pint fresh raspberries, picked over carefully**
Confectioners' sugar

1. Brush the bottom of the tart shell lightly with currant glaze. Arrange the raspberries in the tart shell, mounding them slightly in the center.

2. Dab the raspberries carefully with the remaining glaze. Just before serving, sprinkle the edge of the tart with confectioners' sugar.

TOMATO-AVOCADO ASPIC

POTATO-CHEESE SOUFFLÉ

VEGETABLE SALAD SAUTÉ

CHOCOLATE PEARS

This is a menu that can be put together any time of the year, but it is particularly welcome during the winter months when the days are gray and dreary. Everyone's spirits are lifted by the colors and flavors in these vegetable dishes. And for dessert, who can resist a perfectly poached fresh pear encased in rich chocolate? To reduce last-minute frenzy, poach and dip the pears the day before you plan to serve them; and be sure to prepare the tomato aspic far enough ahead to assure proper jelling.

Tomato-Avocado Aspic   SERVES 6

2	Tbs. butter	1	bay leaf
½	cup minced onion	2	Tbs. unflavored gelatin
1	cup coarsely chopped celery leaves		(2 envelopes)
		½	cup chicken stock (p. 207) or canned chicken broth
5	ripe tomatoes, chopped, or a 1-pound can tomatoes and their juice	1	small ripe avocado, peeled and sliced
2½	cups tomato juice		Watercress sprigs for garnish
½	tsp. dried tarragon		

1. Heat the butter in a heavy saucepan. Add the onion and celery leaves and sauté over low heat for 10 minutes.

2. Add the tomatoes, tomato juice, tarragon, and bay leaf. Simmer, covered, for 30 minutes.

3. Sprinkle the gelatin over the chicken stock and let it soften for 10 minutes. Strain the cooked tomato mixture into a large bowl, pressing down hard on the solids. Add the softened gelatin, stirring until it is dissolved. Let the mixture cool over a bowl of ice, then transfer it to a lightly oiled 1½-quart mold. Refrigerate just until syrupy (about 20 minutes). Add the sliced avocado and chill until the aspic is firm, about 5 hours. Unmold onto a serving platter and decorate with watercress sprigs.

Potato-Cheese Soufflé   SERVES 6

If you have never attempted a soufflé before, this is a good one to start with because it always works. You can hold this soufflé in a turned-off oven for up to 10 minutes and it will retain its golden puffiness.

2	cups warm mashed potatoes (about 3 medium potatoes)	¼	pound sharp cheddar cheese, diced
4	Tbs. butter, softened	3	egg whites, stiffly beaten
¼	cup heavy cream		Butter
1	cup grated Parmesan cheese		Fine dry bread crumbs
3	egg yolks		

PREHEAT THE OVEN TO 400°.

1. In a food processor fitted with the metal blade, combine the potatoes, butter, heavy cream, Parmesan cheese, and egg yolks. Process until smooth. Remove the mixture to a large mixing bowl.

2. Stir in the diced cheddar cheese. Gently fold in the beaten egg whites. Turn the mixture into a well-buttered, crumb-coated 1½- or 2-quart soufflé case. Bake in a preheated 400° oven for about 45 minutes. Serve hot.

Vegetable Salad Sauté   SERVES 6

Since the vegetables in this dish are cooked only briefly, they retain their bright colors and crisp textures.

3	Tbs. butter	2	large red bell peppers, seeded and cubed
½	pound broccoli flowerets (about 1½ cups)	1	Tbs. chopped parsley
3	ribs celery sliced thin	1	Tbs. chopped scallions
			Salt and pepper

1. Melt the butter in a large heavy skillet. Add the broccoli, celery, and red pepper. Cook, stirring, over moderate heat for 5 minutes.

2. Stir in the parsley and scallions; cook, covered, over low heat for 4 minutes. Add salt and pepper to taste. Serve hot.

Chocolate Pears   SERVES 6

This is the dessert to serve when you want to end a good meal with an elegant touch. If you have a beautiful round or oval platter, arrange the pears on it and bring it to the table.

6	poached pears (p. 138)	3	oz. sweet butter, softened
4	oz. good quality semisweet chocolate	6	fresh mint leaves

1. Poach the pears according to the directions for poached pears with raspberry sauce. Refrigerate the pears in the poaching liquid until cold.

2. Combine the chocolate and butter in the top half of a double boiler over simmering water. Heat until the chocolate melts, stirring occasionally. Let cool briefly.

3. Dry the pears with paper toweling. Carefully dip each pear in melted chocolate to cover. Refrigerate for 15 minutes and dip the pears a second time. Press a fresh mint leaf to the top of each pear and chill until the chocolate hardens, at least 2 hours.

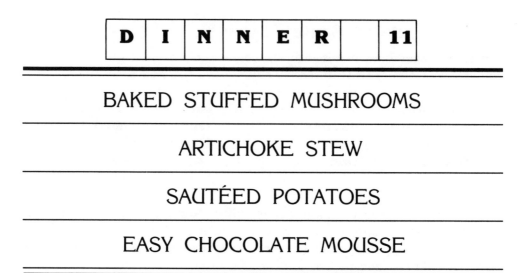

| D | I | N | N | E | R | | 11 |

BAKED STUFFED MUSHROOMS

ARTICHOKE STEW

SAUTÉED POTATOES

EASY CHOCOLATE MOUSSE

These dishes comprise a menu I have often served to guests; it is always well received. The preparation time is considerable, but everything except the sautéed potatoes can be prepared ahead of time. You might like to serve a simple salad of bibb or Boston lettuce preceding the dessert course.

Baked Stuffed Mushrooms   SERVES 6

18	large unblemished mushrooms	¼	cup grated Parmesan cheese
4	Tbs. butter	½	cup chopped prosciutto (optional)
½	cup minced shallots	2	Tbs. heavy cream
¼	cup Madeira	¼	tsp. dried basil
¼	cup minced parsley		Butter
¼	cup fresh bread crumbs		Additional Parmesan cheese
¼	cup grated Swiss cheese		

PREHEAT THE OVEN TO 375°.

1. Wipe the mushrooms clean with a damp cloth. Remove and chop the stems.

2. Heat the butter in a large heavy skillet. Add the shallots and cook, stirring, over low heat until soft. Add the chopped mushroom stems; sauté over medium heat until the mushroom liquid evaporates, about 5 minutes.

3. Add the Madeira and cook until reduced to 1 tablespoon. Remove from the heat and let the mixture cool briefly.

4. Add the parsley, bread crumbs, both cheeses, prosciutto, heavy cream, and basil. Combine the mixture well.

5. Mound the filling into each of the mushroom caps. (May be prepared ahead to this point and refrigerated; bring to room temperature before baking.) Arrange the stuffed mushroom caps in a single layer in a buttered baking dish. Sprinkle with additional Parmesan cheese and bake in a preheated 375° oven for 20 minutes. Serve hot.

Artichoke Stew   SERVES 6

It took many years before I was able to work up the courage to deal with an artichoke. They always looked so beautiful, neatly lined up at the greengrocer's—but making them edible seemed a mystery. Preparing artichokes for cooking takes a bit of doing, but once you've enjoyed the subtle flavor of freshly cooked artichokes, you'll want to serve them often. Follow the directions on pp. 109-10 (artichokes with mustard sauce), but remove and discard all the outer leaves until you reach the tender pale green leaves of the artichoke heart. Using a vegetable peeler or paring knife, trim the base of each artichoke until smooth. Cut the hearts into ½-inch-lengthwise slices. Scoop away the fuzzy choke and drop the cut slices into acidulated water (1 tablespoon lemon juice in a quart of water).

⅓	cup olive oil	4	tomatoes, peeled, seeded, and chopped, or 1 cup canned tomatoes, drained and chopped
½	pound very small white (pearl) onions, peeled		
3	ribs celery, sliced		
	Sliced hearts of 4 large artichokes (see above)	1	Tbs. chopped parsley
		½	tsp. dried basil
1	clove garlic, minced	2	Tbs. drained capers

1. Heat the olive oil in a large heavy casserole. Add the onions and celery. Cook over medium heat 5 minutes, stirring constantly; do not let the vegetables brown.

2. Add the artichoke hearts. Cook, uncovered, over low heat for 10 minutes. Stir occasionally to prevent sticking.

3. Add the garlic, tomatoes, parsley, and basil. Cover and simmer 15 minutes or until the artichokes are tender. (May be prepared ahead and gently reheated.) Just before serving, stir in the capers. Serve hot.

Sautéed Potatoes   SERVES 6

2	pounds new potatoes or boiling potatoes	2	Tbs. oil
		¼	tsp. salt
1	Tbs. butter	1	Tbs. minced parsley

1. Peel and trim the potatoes into small ovals.
2. Heat the butter and oil in a large heavy skillet until foamy. When the foam subsides, add the potatoes and cook over medium heat for 5 or 6 minutes. Shake the pan from time to time to prevent sticking.
3. Sprinkle on the salt, lower the heat, and cover. Cook the potatoes about 20 minutes. They should be evenly and lightly browned. May be kept warm over an asbestos pad for 20 minutes. Sprinkle with parsley before serving.

Easy Chocolate Mousse   SERVES 6

Easy chocolate mousse is just that—total preparation time is about 15 minutes.

6	oz. semisweet chocolate squares	2	Tbs. rum
		½	cup very cold heavy cream
4	egg yolks	4	egg whites, stiffly beaten
2	tsp. sugar		
1	Tbs. coffee extract (1 Tbs. instant coffee dissolved in 1 Tbs. cold water)		

1. Melt the chocolate in the top half of a double boiler over simmering water. Set aside.

2. Beat the egg yolks and sugar together until the mixture is pale yellow. Stir in the melted chocolate, coffee extract, and rum.

3. Whip the cream in a chilled mixing bowl until it is stiff; fold into the melted chocolate.

4. Stir one-fourth of the beaten egg whites into the chocolate mixture to lighten it, then gently fold in the remaining egg whites.

5. Spoon the mousse into individual long-stemmed glasses or a decorative crystal bowl. Refrigerate at least 4 hours or overnight.

DINNER 12

BLACK BEAN SOUP

TOSTADAS with SALSA CRUDA

STUFFED PEPPERS

AVOCADO-ONION SALAD

CRÈME CARAMEL

A thick, richly flavored black bean soup is the ideal beginning for this Mexican dinner. Although the soup requires long cooking, it doesn't need much attention—you can leave it simmering on the back burner and pretty much forget about it.

Your preparation schedule for this dinner should look like this: (1) The day before, prepare the crème caramel. (2) Morning of the dinner, make the black bean soup and *salsa cruda*. (3) Three hours before serving, prepare the stuffed peppers for baking. (4) Half an hour before serving, make the *tostadas* and avocado-onion salad.

Black Bean Soup   SERVES 6

¾   pound dried black beans
2   quarts chicken stock (p. 207)
    or 4 cups of canned chicken
    broth and 4 cups of water
¼   cup vegetable oil
1½ cups chopped onions
½   cup chopped scallions
2   large cloves garlic, crushed

1   bay leaf
½   tsp. dried oregano
⅛   tsp. dried hot red pepper
    flakes
1   Tbs. dry sherry
    Minced onion for garnish
    Chopped coriander (Chinese
    parsley) for garnish

1. Rinse the beans and put them in a large kettle with the stock. Bring to a boil. Remove from the heat and let stand, partially covered, for 1 hour.

2. Heat the oil in a large skillet; add the onions and scallions and cook until translucent. Add to the soup kettle along with the garlic, bay leaf, oregano, and red pepper. Bring to a boil, reduce the heat, and simmer, partially covered, until the beans are tender (this can take up to 3 hours).

3. For a very thick soup, remove and puree all the beans in batches in a food processor or blender along with some of the soup liquid. If you prefer a thinner soup, puree only half the beans. Return the puree to the soup and heat through. Add the sherry. Serve in small bowls garnished with minced onion and coriander; accompany with *tostadas* and *salsa cruda* (recipes below).

Tostadas with Salsa Cruda   SERVES 6

12 corn tortillas

2   cups vegetable oil

Tortillas are available canned or frozen in specialty food shops and in many supermarkets. Cut the tortillas into quarters and fry them in batches in hot oil; they become crisp and golden in a matter of seconds. Drain on paper toweling. Serve with *salsa cruda.*

Salsa Cruda

This traditional Mexican condiment, a spicy uncooked tomato sauce, is found on virtually every Mexican table. The spiciest *salsa* is made with canned *serrano* chiles (available at shops specializing in Mexican and Latin American foods); if you like a milder taste, substitute dried hot red pepper flakes.

2	large ripe tomatoes, peeled, seeded, and chopped	1	Tbs. minced scallion
1	canned *serrano* chile, chopped, or ¼ tsp. dried hot red pepper flakes	1	Tbs. minced fresh coriander (Chinese parsley)
1	small onion, minced		Salt and freshly ground pepper to taste

Combine all the ingredients in a medium mixing bowl; refrigerate until serving time.

Note: The blender or food processor is not recommended for this recipe since it would produce a very watery sauce.

Stuffed Peppers   SERVES 6

6	medium red or green bell peppers	½	cup tomato juice
4	Tbs. butter	1½	cups grated cheddar cheese
1	cup rice	3	Tbs. chopped coriander (Chinese parsley, optional)
1½	cups water		
1	medium onion, chopped		

PREHEAT THE OVEN TO 350°.

1. Cut the peppers in half lengthwise and remove the pith and seeds. Blanch the peppers in boiling water for 8 minutes. Drain and set aside.

2. Heat 2 tablespoons of the butter in a saucepan; add the rice, stirring until it is coated with butter. Add the water, bring to a boil, reduce the heat, and simmer, covered, for 17 minutes. Reserve.

3. In a skillet heat the remaining 2 tablespoons butter. Add the chopped onion and cook until translucent. Remove from the heat; stir in the reserved

rice and remaining ingredients and combine well. Fill the pepper halves with the rice mixture. (May be prepared ahead to this point.) Arrange the peppers in a lightly oiled baking dish. Bake in a preheated 350° oven for 20 minutes.

Avocado-Onion Salad   SERVES 6

3	medium avocados, peeled and sliced	1	Tbs. lemon juice
1	medium red onion, sliced	4	Tbs. olive oil
	Salt and pepper	¼	tsp. dried oregano

1. Arrange alternating slices of avocado and onion on a decorative platter. Sprinkle with salt and pepper to taste.
2. Whisk together the lemon juice and olive oil; stir in the oregano. Spoon the dressing over the salad.

Crème Caramel   SERVES 6

¾	cup sugar	2½	cups milk, scalded
2	Tbs. water	½	tsp. vanilla extract
3	eggs		

PREHEAT THE OVEN TO 350°.
1. Heat ½ cup of the sugar with the water in a small heavy skillet. Stir constantly until the sugar melts and turns golden. Line each of 6 half-cup custard molds with the caramel. Let cool slightly.
2. Beat the eggs lightly with the remaining ¼ cup sugar. Slowly stir in the scalded milk. Add the vanilla.
3. Carefully pour the mixture into the prepared custard molds. Place the molds in a pan and add enough boiling water to come halfway up the sides of the molds. Bake in a preheated 350° oven for 50 minutes to 1 hour or until a knife inserted down the middle of the custard comes out clean.
4. Cool to room temperature, then refrigerate. Serve chilled or at room temperature, unmolded.

DINNER 13

SPINACH-MUSHROOM SALAD

RICE-STUFFED TOMATOES

PUREED ZUCCHINI

STRAWBERRIES CHANTILLY

This is the sort of casual, light-tasting meal that makes the best summer fare. It's easy to prepare and you'll love the way the bright colors enliven your table. If you would like a slightly fuller menu, add the cold cucumber-yogurt soup (p. 83) and serve a simple green salad in place of the spinach-mushroom salad.

Spinach-Mushroom Salad   SERVES 4

This is a very popular salad and justly so. Texture plays an important part here; be sure to use firm crisp mushrooms and fresh unwilted spinach. Spinach-mushroom salad on its own is a good light lunch.

1	pound fresh, crisp spinach, rinsed and cut into bite-sized pieces
¼	pound fresh, unblemished mushrooms, sliced
2	Tbs. chopped shallots

2	Tbs. tarragon vinegar
¼	cup vegetable oil
¼	cup olive oil
	Salt and freshly ground black pepper to taste

60

1. Pat the spinach dry with paper toweling. Place in a large salad bowl. Add the sliced mushrooms and shallots.

2. Whisk together the vinegar, oils, and salt and pepper. Just before serving, toss the salad with the vinaigrette dressing.

Rice-stuffed Tomatoes   SERVES 4

8	medium, firm, ripe tomatoes	1	cup cooked rice
½	tsp. dried basil	4	Tbs. olive oil
¼	tsp. dried thyme		Salt and pepper to taste
1	large clove garlic, minced		

PREHEAT THE OVEN TO 375°.

1. Cut the tops off the tomatoes and reserve them. Gently squeeze out the seeds and juice. Remove and chop the tomato pulp; set aside.

2. In a mixing bowl combine the chopped tomato pulp, basil, thyme, garlic, cooked rice, and 2 tablespoons of the olive oil. Add the salt and pepper. Mix well and fill each tomato with the mixture. May be prepared ahead to this point.

3. Oil a rectangular baking dish with the remaining 2 tablespoons of olive oil. Arrange the tomatoes in the dish and cover with the reserved tops. Bake in a preheated 375° oven for 20 minutes or until the tomatoes are heated through but still hold their shape. Remove to a serving dish and allow the tomatoes to cool for 10 minutes before serving.

Pureed Zucchini   SERVES 4

1¼	pounds zucchini, cut into ¼-inch slices		Salt and pepper
2	Tbs. butter	1	Tbs. freshly grated Parmesan cheese

1. Drop the zucchini into a saucepan of rapidly boiling water. Cook, covered, for 4 minutes. Drain immediately and pat dry with paper toweling.

2. Puree the zucchini in a blender or food processor. Heat the butter in the saucepan, add the pureed zucchini, salt and pepper to taste, and toss just until heated through.

3. Serve the zucchini in a warmed vegetable dish and sprinkle on the Parmesan cheese.

Strawberries Chantilly   SERVES 4

Nothing could be easier than sweet, ripe strawberries served with lightly flavored whipped cream. This is always a warm-weather favorite.

1½	pints strawberries, rinsed and hulled	1	to 2 Tbs. confectioners' sugar
1	cup heavy cream	½	tsp. vanilla extract

1. If the berries are very large, cut them in half lengthwise; otherwise, leave whole. Refrigerate until serving time.

2. Beat the cream in a large well-chilled mixing bowl. Add the sugar and continue beating until the cream forms soft peaks. Do not overbeat. If you wish to keep the chantilly in the refrigerator for several hours, place in a fine mesh sieve over a bowl. Stir in the vanilla just before serving.

3. Arrange the strawberries on each of 4 plates with a generous serving of flavored cream on the side.

CELERY RÉMOULADE

SWISS CRÊPES with MUSHROOM SAUCE

HOT DILLED CUCUMBER

GINGER PEARS

This is an elegant menu that could well be the perfect choice for an important dinner party. Happily, the first course and dessert can be prepared the day before, leaving you unharried at dinner time.

Celery Rémoulade   SERVES 6

The celery in this dish is knob celery, also known as celery root or celeriac. It is a hard, knobby root vegetable that has long been a great favorite in Europe. Celery *rémoulade* is a classic French appetizer.

2	pounds celery root		1	tsp. lemon juice
2	Tbs. white wine vinegar		2	Tbs. Dijon mustard
	Salt and pepper		3	Tbs. heavy cream
1	cup homemade mayonnaise (p. 205)			Watercress sprigs

1. Peel the celery root and cut it into julienne strips, or use a food processor fitted with the julienne blade.

2. Plunge the julienne celery root into a large quantity of rapidly boiling water for 20 seconds. Drain immediately under cold running water. Pat dry with paper toweling.

3. Place the celery root in a large bowl and toss with vinegar, salt, and pepper.

4. Prepare the *rémoulade* sauce by combining the mayonnaise with the lemon juice, mustard, and cream; mix well. Stir the *rémoulade* sauce into the celery root, tossing to coat the pieces well. May be prepared a day ahead and refrigerated. Serve on individual plates garnished with watercress sprigs.

Swiss Crêpes with Mushroom Sauce   SERVES 6

THE CRÊPE BATTER:

Add ½ cup finely grated Swiss cheese to the basic crêpe batter (p. 203). Make 12 crêpes. Keep the crêpes covered with a damp cloth until you are ready to use them.

THE MUSHROOM SAUCE:

3	Tbs. butter	¾	cup heavy cream
2	Tbs. chopped shallots	2	tsp. dry sherry (optional)
1½	pounds mushrooms, sliced thin		

1. Heat the butter in a large skillet. Add the shallots and cook until soft. Add the mushrooms and sauté for about 5 minutes. Pour in the heavy cream and cook over moderately low heat for 20 minutes or until the mushrooms have absorbed some of the cream and the mixture has a saucelike consistency. Stir in the sherry if desired. Transfer the sauce to a small pan and keep warm over simmering water.

2. Roll up the reserved crêpes and arrange them in a buttered baking dish. Cover the dish with a damp kitchen towel (to prevent crêpes from drying out while in the oven); heat through for 15 minutes. Serve the crêpes on warmed plates with the mushroom sauce spooned over them.

Hot Dilled Cucumber   SERVES 6

Instead of relegating cucumber to the salad bowl, try cooking it gently in butter and serving it hot with fresh chopped dill.

3	large cucumbers		Salt and pepper to taste
3	Tbs. butter	2	Tbs. fresh chopped dill

1. Peel the cucumbers. Cut them in half lengthwise and scoop out the seeds. Cut the halves into ½-inch slices.
2. Melt the butter in a heavy saucepan over low heat. Add the sliced cucumber, cover, and cook over low heat for 10 minutes. Add salt and pepper and stir in the dill. Remove to a warm vegetable dish and serve immediately.

Ginger Pears   SERVES 6

Fresh pears poached in a lightly spiced syrup.

6	firm, ripe pears	¾	cup sugar
	Juice of ½ lemon	2	tsp. freshly grated ginger
4	cups water		root

1. Peel and core the pears. Cut them into quarters. Sprinkle with lemon juice to prevent discoloration.

2. Make a poaching syrup by combining the remaining ingredients. Bring to a boil and simmer, covered, for 20 minutes.

3. Drop the pears into the syrup and simmer, covered, for 10 to 15 minutes or until just tender. Allow the pears to cool in the syrup before refrigerating. Serve well chilled with a spoonful or two of ginger syrup.

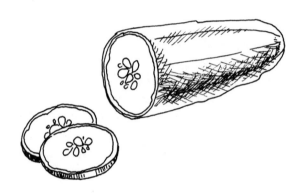

FETA with OLIVES

PAPRIKA VEGETABLE STEW

BUTTERED NOODLES

MARINATED CUCUMBER SALAD

APRICOTS in COGNAC (PP. 35-36)

This menu, with middle European overtones, would certainly be welcome on a frosty winter day. The star of the meal is a savory vegetable stew heady with the aroma of paprika and wine.

Feta with Olives   SERVES 6

1	pound feta cheese, cubed		Freshly ground black pepper
1½	cups pitted Greek olives		to taste
1	small red onion, sliced thin	¼	cup olive oil
¼	tsp. dried oregano		

In a large mixing bowl combine all the ingredients except the olive oil. Just before serving, add the oil and toss gently.

Paprika Vegetable Stew   SERVES 6

Do not be put off by the long list of ingredients in this dish. They are all readily available, and once you've put the stew in the oven, you can relax. I've suggested plain buttered noodles as a good accompaniment to the stew; bulgur pilaf (p. 35) would work well with this dish too.

¼	cup olive oil	12	whole baby carrots, peeled
1	red bell pepper, cut into 1-inch squares	1	rutabaga, about 1 pound, peeled and cubed
1	green bell pepper, cut into 1-inch squares	1	tart apple (Granny Smith or Greening), peeled and cubed
1	medium red onion, thickly sliced	2	cups dry red wine
2	cloves garlic, chopped	¼	cup minced parsley
¼	cup chopped shallots	2	Tbs. minced fresh dill
2	bay leaves	½	tsp. sugar
1	pound boiling potatoes, peeled and cut into 1-inch squares	1	Tbs. mild paprika
4	tomatoes, peeled, seeded, and chopped, or 1 cup canned tomatoes, drained and chopped		Yogurt

PREHEAT THE OVEN TO 350°

1. Heat the olive oil in a large heavy casserole. Add the next 6 ingredients and cook, stirring, over moderate heat for 5 minutes.

2. Add the remaining vegetables and the apple and cook for 5 minutes. Add the wine, herbs, sugar, and paprika. Stir the mixture well, cover the casserole, and transfer it to a preheated 350° oven. Bake the stew for 1½ hours. Serve hot with yogurt.

Buttered Noodles   SERVES 6

¾	pound broad egg noodles		Salt to taste
3	Tbs. softened butter	1	tsp. caraway seeds (optional)

1. Cook the noodles in 3 quarts boiling water until tender, about 8 minutes. Drain well.

2. Turn the noodles into a large warmed serving dish. Stir in the softened butter and salt. If desired, sprinkle on the caraway seeds.

Marinated Cucumber Salad   SERVES 6

If you find Kirby ("pickle") cucumbers, use them in this recipe. Their firmer texture gives the salad just the right crunch. If Kirbys are not available, regular cucumbers may be substituted.

5	medium cucumbers, peeled and seeded		Freshly ground black pepper to taste
	Salt	1/3	cup red onion, sliced paper thin
1/2	cup white wine vinegar		
2	tsp mild paprika	2	Tbs. minced fresh dill
1/2	tsp. sugar		Pinch of hot red pepper flakes (optional)

1. Cut the cucumbers into very thin slices. Salt the slices liberally and let them drain in a colander for 30 minutes. Rinse briefly and pat dry with paper toweling.

2. In a small mixing bowl combine the vinegar, paprika, sugar, and black pepper. Stir in the onion, dill, and hot red pepper if you are using it. Let the dressing rest for at least half an hour. Pour the dressing over the cucumbers and refrigerate for an hour or more before serving.

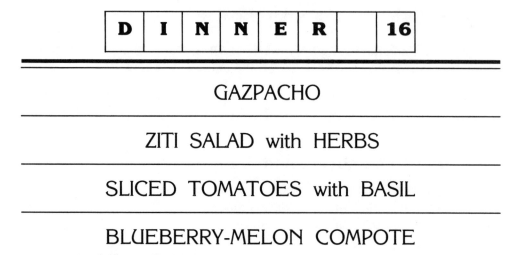

GAZPACHO

ZITI SALAD with HERBS

SLICED TOMATOES with BASIL

BLUEBERRY-MELON COMPOTE

This refreshing warm-weather menu makes the greatest use of summer vegetables at their peak. The gazpacho, ziti, and dessert may all be prepared ahead and refrigerated. Slice the tomatoes and garnish them with basil just before you are ready to serve them.

Gazpacho   SERVES 6

Everyone has a favorite gazpacho recipe; this is mine. A little more or less of any of the ingredients won't affect the results; it will still be delicious. Be sure to serve the soup very cold. I usually put it in the freezer for half an hour before serving.

2	large ripe tomatoes, peeled and seeded	¼	cup olive oil
1	large red bell pepper, seeded	3	cups chilled chicken stock (p. 207) or 1½ cups canned chicken broth and 1½ cups water
1	large clove garlic, peeled		
1	medium red onion, peeled		
1	medium cucumber, peeled and seeded	½	cup chilled tomato juice
		½	tsp. paprika
½	cup mixed fresh herbs such as parsley, basil, chives, and dill	1	Tbs. lime juice
			Salt and pepper to taste

1. In a blender or food processor, puree in batches the tomatoes, pepper, garlic, onion, cucumber, and mixed herbs. Set aside in a large mixing bowl.

2. Slowly whisk in the olive oil. Stir in the remaining ingredients. Chill well.

Ziti Salad with Herbs   SERVES 6

In recent years cold pasta salads have become very popular. They taste good, they're easy to prepare, and they always look pretty. This salad can be made with either ziti or rigatoni.

1	pound ziti	1	red bell pepper, cut in julienne strips
3	Tbs. red wine vinegar		
¾	cup olive oil	3	slices prosciutto, shredded (optional)
½	tsp. Dijon mustard		
¼	cup chopped scallions	2	Tbs. freshly grated Parmesan cheese
¼	cup chopped dill		
¼	cup chopped parsley		

1. Cook the ziti in a large kettle of boiling salted water for 10 to 12 minutes or until *al dente* (firm to the bite; do not overcook). Drain well in a colander. Set aside in a large mixing bowl.

2. In a small bowl whisk together the vinegar, olive oil, and mustard. Pour the dressing over the ziti. Add the remaining ingredients and toss well. Serve at room temperature.

Sliced Tomatoes with Basil   SERVES 6

6   **medium, ripe tomatoes,**   **Salt and pepper to taste**
         sliced   **2**   **Tbs. olive oil**
2   **Tbs. fresh chopped basil**

Arrange the tomatoes in a circular pattern on a large platter and sprinkle with basil; add salt and pepper. Dribble on the olive oil. Serve at room temperature.

Blueberry-Melon Compote   SERVES 6

3   **cups melon balls (cantaloupe**   **Juice of 2 freshly squeezed**
         and honeydew)   **oranges**
1   **cup fresh blueberries, rinsed**
         and picked over

In a large mixing bowl combine the melon balls and blueberries. Pour the orange juice over the fruit and chill thoroughly.

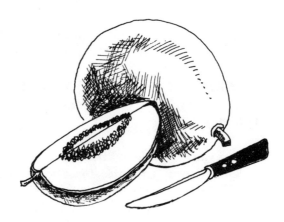

MARINATED EGGPLANT

SPINACH-CHEESE PIE

BAKED TOMATOES

EASY CHOCOLATE MOUSSE (PP. 54-55)

You will find this menu particularly well suited to late supper or after-theater dinner entertaining. The first course, main course, and dessert are all prepared ahead of time. Preparation time for the tomatoes, which is last minute, is about 7 minutes; baking time, 20 minutes.

Marinated Eggplant   SERVES 6

THE EGGPLANT:

**3   small eggplants, about
      6 inches long
      Salt**

THE MARINADE:

2	cups water	¼	tsp. dried thyme
⅓	cup olive oil	¼	tsp. dried celery seed
¼	cup lemon juice	1	large clove garlic, unpeeled
4	parsley stems		Salt and pepper to taste
⅛	tsp. dried fennel seed		

1. Remove the stems from the eggplants and cut them into ¼-inch-thick slices. Sprinkle with salt and place in a colander with a weight on them (a heavy pot will do). Let the eggplant drain this way for 30 minutes.

2. Place all the ingredients for the marinade in a saucepan that will later accommodate the sliced eggplant. Bring to a boil, cover, and simmer for 10 minutes.

3. Dry the eggplant slices between paper towels and add them to the marinade. Cover and simmer for 8 minutes. The eggplant should be crisp-tender. Remove the eggplant from the pan and set aside. Boil the remaining marinade until it is reduced to about ⅓ cup. Strain and pour over the eggplant. Serve chilled on a bed of lettuce.

Spinach-Cheese Pie   SERVES 6

This pie is a variation on the Greek *spanakopitta*. It is made with the spinach-cheese filling that appears on page 96 (spinach-stuffed crêpes) and baked in an 8-inch round tin lined with either phyllo or strudel leaves. The result is a beautiful pie—puffed, golden, and delicious.

Phyllo dough is now widely available frozen in most supermarkets. Be sure to follow the package instructions for thawing. Once you have removed the phyllo leaves from their package, keep them covered with a damp cloth to prevent them from drying out.

	Spinach-cheese filling (p. 96)	4	ounces (one stick) melted
4	phyllo or strudel leaves		butter

PREHEAT THE OVEN TO 350°

1. Prepare the spinach-cheese filling and set aside.

2. Working quickly, stack the phyllo leaves on a dampened kitchen towel and fold them in half lengthwise; fold in half again widthwise. You should have a square about 10 inches by 9 inches.

3. Using an 8-inch round tin as a guide, cut the folded phyllo leaves into a circle slightly larger than the tin. You now have 16 round leaves.

4. Butter the tin and place one phyllo leaf in it. Brush with melted butter. Repeat this process until you have used 8 leaves.

5. Add the spinach filling, smoothing it over the pastry. Cover with the remaining phyllo circles, brushing each with melted butter.

6. With a sharp knife score the top layers into six equal wedges. Bake in a preheated 350° oven for 30 minutes or until puffed and golden. The fully baked pie may be refrigerated overnight; to reheat, place in a 350° oven for 20 minutes.

Baked Tomatoes   SERVES 6

6	firm ripe tomatoes		Freshly ground black pepper
1	large clove garlic		to taste
1	large shallot	½	cup dry bread crumbs
3	Tbs. minced basil or parsley	2	Tbs. olive oil

PREHEAT THE OVEN TO 350°

1. Remove the stem ends from the tomatoes. Cut the tomatoes in half and gently squeeze out the juice and seeds.

2. Put the remaining ingredients in a food processor or blender and process until just blended together.

3. Press a tablespoon of the herbed crumbs into each tomato half. Arrange the tomatoes in an oiled oven-proof baking dish; bake for 20 minutes in a preheated 350° oven. Serve hot.

FRESH TOMATO-BASIL SOUP

ZUCCHINI FRITTERS

MOZZARELLA-OLIVE SALAD

LEMON SOUFFLÉ TART

For those of you with your own gardens, here are several recipes to help solve the problem of what to do with all those tomatoes, so much zucchini, and basil that never seems to stop growing.

Fresh Tomato-Basil Soup   SERVES 4

Tomato and basil are always a welcome summer duo. The addition of a small amount of dried fennel seed gives the soup a very refreshing flavor. If it's a very warm summer night, serve the soup well chilled. In September when there is a hint of fall chill in the air, serve the soup hot.

2	Tbs. olive oil	2	Tbs. fresh chopped basil or ½ tsp. dried
1	large stalk celery, chopped		
1	medium onion, chopped	¼	tsp. dried fennel seeds
1	large carrot, scraped and chopped	4	cups chicken stock (p. 207) or 2 cups canned chicken broth and 2 cups water
1	clove garlic, chopped		
2	pounds ripe tomatoes, peeled, seeded, and chopped		Additional basil for garnish

1. Heat the olive oil in a large heavy saucepan. Add the celery, onion, carrot, and garlic. Cook over low heat, stirring, until the vegetables are soft.

2. Add the tomatoes, basil, fennel, and chicken stock. Bring to a boil, reduce the heat, and simmer, covered, for 30 minutes.

3. Remove the solids from the soup and puree in a blender or food processor. Return the puree to the liquid and heat through. Garnish each serving with chopped basil.

Zucchini Fritters   SERVES 4

2½	pounds zucchini	1	egg, lightly beaten
	Salt	¼	cup freshly grated Parmesan
⅓	cup dry unflavored bread		cheese
	crumbs		Flour for dredging
½	tsp. dried basil	½	cup vegetable oil
1	clove garlic, minced		

1. Shred the zucchini using either a hand-held grater or a food processor fitted with the shredding blade. Salt the zucchini liberally and let drain in a colander for about half an hour. Rinse briefly under running water. Twist the zucchini in a kitchen towel to remove the moisture—it must be dry to fry properly.

2. Put the zucchini in a large mixing bowl and add the bread crumbs, basil, garlic, egg, and Parmesan cheese, mixing well to incorporate everything. Shape the mixture into patties about 3 inches in diameter; dredge lightly with flour.

3. Heat the vegetable oil in a large heavy skillet; when it is quite hot, add the fritters and fry in batches until browned on both sides. Drain on paper towels. If not served immediately, the fritters can be kept warm for about 20 minutes in a 300° oven.

Mozzarella-Olive Salad   SERVES 4

Do not attempt to make this dish unless you can obtain a good-quality, fresh, whole-milk mozzarella. The salty, plastic encased, rubbery cheese sold as mozzarella in the supermarket really won't work. Most well-stocked cheese stores and specialty food shops now carry fresh mozzarella.

1	pound fresh mozzarella	½	tsp. dried oregano
1	cup oil-cured or Niçoise olives, pitted		Freshly ground black pepper
		¼	cup good, fruity olive oil

Cut the mozzarella into narrow strips about 2 inches long. Combine the cheese and olives in a medium-sized mixing bowl. Sprinkle on the oregano. Add black pepper to taste and toss with olive oil. Serve the salad at room temperature.

Lemon Soufflé Tart   SERVES 4–6

This is a wonderful, light pastry with a very tart, refreshing taste.

1	partially baked 9-inch sweet tart shell (p. 203), cooled	2½	Tbs. butter, cut into small pieces
3	large eggs, separated	⅓	cup superfine sugar
¼	cup granulated sugar		Confectioners' sugar
½	cup plus 1 Tbs. lemon juice		

1. In a mixing bowl beat together the egg yolks and ¼ cup sugar until the mixture is pale yellow and forms a ribbon. Stir in ½ cup lemon juice.
2. Pour the mixture into a heavy-bottomed saucepan, add the butter, and stir constantly over moderately low heat until the mixture thickens. Pour into a bowl and chill for about half an hour.
PREHEAT THE OVEN TO 375°.
3. In a copper mixing bowl beat the egg whites until they form soft peaks. Slowly add the instant-dissolving sugar in a stream. Add the remaining tablespoon of lemon juice and beat the mixture until firm and shiny.
4. Gently fold the egg-white mixture into the chilled egg-yolk mixture; turn it into the partially baked tart shell. Bake on the top shelf of a preheated 375° oven for 20 minutes or until the tart is puffed and lightly browned. Remove to a rack to cool. The tart will sink slightly as it cools. Serve at room temperature dusted with confectioners' sugar.

DINNER 19

JULIENNE CARROT SALAD

SPINACH-RICOTTA SOUFFLÉ

SAUTÉED MUSHROOMS with SHALLOTS

CHOUX à la CRÈME with RICH CHOCOLATE SAUCE

Be prepared for a steady stream of compliments when you serve this dinner with its exciting array of colors, textures, and flavors.

Julienne Carrot Salad   SERVES 4

This is one of the best salads I have ever eaten. The walnut-oil dressing is what makes it so special. Do not be tempted to make the salad without walnut oil (which admittedly is expensive). If you do, you'll miss the whole point of this salad. The distinctive nut-flavored dressing works wonderfully with the crunchy texture of carrots.

1	pound carrots, scraped and cut in julienne strips	¼	cup peanut oil
2	Tbs. lemon juice	1	tsp. Dijon mustard
¼	cup walnut oil	3	Tbs. finely minced fresh dill

1. Plunge the carrots into a large pot of boiling water for 30 seconds. Drain immediately under cold running water. Pat dry with paper toweling. Set aside.

2. In a small bowl whisk together the lemon juice, oils, and mustard. Stir in the dill and pour the dressing over the carrots. Toss well. Refrigerate until serving time.

Spinach-Ricotta Soufflé   SERVES 4

This soufflé does not puff up quite as much as a traditional spinach soufflé because it is not made with a cooked flour-sauce base. It is, nonetheless, airy and delicious and easy to prepare since the sauce base is eliminated.

3	Tbs. butter	2	large eggs, lightly beaten
2	Tbs. minced shallots or onions	½	cup grated Parmesan cheese
1	cup cooked spinach, drained and chopped	4	egg whites, stiffly beaten
1	pound ricotta		Softened butter
			Fine dry bread crumbs

PREHEAT THE OVEN TO 375°.

1. Heat the butter in a medium skillet. Add the shallots or onions and cook until wilted. Wring the spinach in a kitchen towel to remove excess moisture, add it to the skillet, and cook, stirring to evaporate any remaining moisture. Set aside to cool slightly.

2. In a mixing bowl combine the ricotta, eggs, and Parmesan cheese. Stir in the reserved spinach.

3. Stir a quarter of the stiffly beaten egg whites into the spinach-cheese mixture to lighten it. Gently fold in the remaining egg whites.

4. Butter the bottom and sides of a 1½-quart soufflé dish and sprinkle with bread crumbs. Turn the soufflé mixture into the prepared dish and bake in a preheated 375° oven for 40 minutes or until puffed and golden. Serve immediately.

Sautéed Mushrooms with Shallots   SERVES 4

⅓   cup vegetable oil
1   pound fresh small
     mushrooms, stems trimmed

1   Tbs. butter
1½   Tbs. minced shallots
1½   Tbs. chopped parsley

1. Heat the oil in a large heavy skillet (cast iron is ideal). When the oil is very hot, add the mushrooms and cook, stirring and tossing, until the mushrooms are lightly browned.
2. Drain the mushrooms in a sieve. Discard the oil in the skillet.
3. Melt the butter in the skillet; add the shallots, mushrooms, and parsley. Cook, tossing, over high heat for 1 minute. Serve hot.

Choux à la Crème   SERVES 4

Sweet, airy, cream-filled puffs served with rich chocolate sauce make a spectacular dessert presentation.

4   cream puffs (see p. 204)
¾   cup heavy cream
1½   Tbs. confectioners' sugar (or
     more, to taste)

½   tsp. vanilla extract or rum

Beat the cream in a large chilled mixing bowl over ice water; use chilled beaters or a chilled whisk. Add the sugar and vanilla and continue beating until the cream is firm and holds soft peaks. The whipped cream may be stored in the refrigerator for an hour. Fill each puff with flavored cream and serve with rich chocolate sauce.

Rich Chocolate Sauce   MAKES ABOUT 1½ CUPS

Be sure to use very good quality bittersweet chocolate for this sauce (I use Lindt brand bittersweet chocolate with vanilla).

**10 ounces bittersweet
chocolate, chopped**
1 cup heavy cream

1. Put the chopped chocolate in a large mixing bowl. Set aside.
2. Bring the cream to a full boil in a heavy saucepan. Immediately pour it over the chopped chocolate. Stir well. In a matter of seconds you will have a very smooth, shiny, thick sauce. Serve it warm or at room temperature. Leftover sauce may be refrigerated for up to a month. Reheat over very low flame to spreadable consistency. This sauce is excellent with poached pears or over ice cream.

D I N N E R 20

ICY CUCUMBER-YOGURT SOUP

TURKISH EGGPLANT

CRACKED WHEAT SALAD

PITA with HERB BUTTER

BLUEBERRY TART

This is a "do ahead" dinner that stylishly ushers in early summer. If blueberries are not available, substitute the lemon soufflé tart on page 78.

Icy Cucumber-Yogurt Soup   SERVES 4

Cool, refreshing soup is always a welcome start to a summer dinner. Be sure to give the soup adequate chilling time; it should be served very cold.

2	Tbs. butter		2	cups chicken stock (p. 207)
¼	cup chopped onion			or 1 cup canned chicken
3	cups cucumber, peeled,			broth and 1 cup water
	seeded, and chopped (about			Freshly ground black pepper
	2 large cucumbers)			to taste
1	cup watercress, including		¼	tsp. ground cumin
	stems, packed		1	cup yogurt
			2	Tbs. fresh chopped dill

1. Heat the butter in a large heavy sauce pan. Add the onion and cook over low heat until soft.

2. Add the remaining ingredients except the yogurt and dill. Bring to a boil and simmer, covered, for 20 minutes or until the cucumber is soft. Remove the solids from the soup and purée in a blender or food processor. Return the purée to the soup and refrigerate at least 6 hours. Before serving, gradually stir in the yogurt and garnish with chopped dill.

Turkish Eggplant   SERVES 4

It is difficult to decide which of the world's cuisines does the most delicious things with eggplant. There are so many wonderful ways to prepare it. The French, Italians, Orientals, and Near Easterners all have their special eggplant dishes and they're all good! In this dish the addition of allspice and currants gives the eggplant a decidedly Near Eastern flavor.

4	small eggplants, about ½ pound each, green stems removed	3	Tbs. currants
			Freshly ground black pepper to taste
	Salt	½	tsp. ground allspice
3	Tbs. olive oil	2	Tbs. chopped parsley
3	medium onions, chopped		Additional olive oil
4	medium tomatoes, peeled, seeded, and chopped, or 1-pound can of Italian tomatoes, drained	1	large clove garlic, peeled, crushed
		1	bay leaf

1. Score the skin of each eggplant all around, making 5 or 6 deep lengthwise cuts. Take care not to cut all the way through. Sprinkle the eggplants with salt, forcing some of it into the cuts. Place the eggplants in a colander with a weight on them (a heavy pot will do). Let them drain this way for 30 minutes.

2. Heat the 3 tablespoons of olive oil in a medium-sized heavy skillet. Add the onions and cook until soft. Add the tomatoes, currants, black pepper,

allspice, and parsley. Cook the mixture over low heat until it is quite thick, about 30 minutes. Set aside until cool.

PREHEAT THE OVEN TO 350°

3. Dry the eggplants with paper toweling and fill the scored flesh with the tomato-onion mixture. Any leftover filling can be added to the casserole in which the eggplants are baked.

4. Choose an oven-proof casserole that will hold the eggplants without crowding. Pour in enough olive oil to cover the eggplants by half. Add the crushed garlic and bay leaf. Cover the casserole and bake in a preheated 350° oven for 1¼ hours. Remove from the oven; let the eggplants cool in the oil. To serve, drain off the oil and cut each eggplant in half lengthwise. May be served at room temperature or chilled.

Cracked Wheat Salad   SERVES 4–6

This flavorful Middle Eastern salad is made with bulgur, which is widely available in specialty food shops and in many supermarkets. It's a fine alternative to rice with many main course dishes; it also makes an excellent appetizer.

1	cup cracked wheat (bulgur)	¼	cup chopped mint leaves
½	cup chopped onions	2	medium tomatoes, cubed
½	cup chopped scallions,		Salt and pepper to taste
	including green tops	¼	cup lemon juice
1½	cups chopped Italian parsley	⅔	cup olive oil

1. Place the cracked wheat in a large mixing bowl and cover with cold water by 2 inches. Let it soak for 1 hour. It will double in bulk. Drain in a sieve, pressing out as much water as possible.

2. Return the cracked wheat to the mixing bowl. Add the onions, chopped scallions, parsley, mint leaves, tomatoes, and salt and pepper. Mix well.

3. In a small bowl whisk together the lemon juice and olive oil. Pour over the salad and toss gently. You may serve the salad chilled, but it tastes better at room temperature.

Pita with Herb Butter   SERVES 4

4	ounces butter (1 stick, softened	1	small clove garlic, crushed Salt and pepper to taste
1	Tbs. minced parsley	3	loaves pita
2	tsp. minced scallions		
1	tsp. lemon juice		

1. Make the herb butter. In a small bowl cream together the butter, parsley, scallions, lemon juice, and garlic. Add salt and pepper. Refrigerate. May be prepared ahead to this point. To facilitate spreading, let the butter stand at room temperature for 15 minutes before using.

PREHEAT THE OVEN TO 500°.

2. Cut the pita loaves in half horizontally; separate the halves into 2 pieces (you now have 12 pieces). Spread each piece with herb butter and arrange the pita on a large baking sheet. Bake on the top shelf of a preheated 500° oven for 5 minutes or until lightly browned around the edges. Serve hot.

Blueberry Tart   SERVES 4–6

1	pint fresh blueberries	1	fully baked 9-inch sweet tart shell (see p. 202)
1	Tbs. sugar		Confectioners' sugar
1	Tbs. lemon juice		
½	cup red currant jelly		

1. Rinse the berries and pick them over carefully.

2. Combine the sugar, lemon juice, and jelly in a small saucepan. Bring the mixture to a boil over medium heat. Away from the heat, carefully stir in the blueberries. Fill the pastry shell with the blueberry mixture. May be prepared up to 3 hours ahead to this point. Do not refrigerate. Just before serving, dust the edge of the tart with confectioners' sugar.

CREAMY CARROT SOUP

GRATIN of CELERY ROOT

HERBED WILD RICE

ENDIVE-WATERCRESS SALAD

ORANGES GRAND MARNIER

Put family or friends in a holiday mood with this special fall/winter menu. Sliced celery root, baked under a blanket of Swiss cheese and bread crumbs, is accompanied by slender grains of herb-flavored wild rice. Round out the dinner with velvety carrot soup, a crisp salad, and classic oranges Grand Marnier.

Creamy Carrot Soup   SERVES 4

2   Tbs. butter
2   Tbs. chopped shallots or onions
1   pound carrots, scraped and coarsely chopped
1½ Tbs. flour

4   cups hot chicken stock (p. 207) or 2 cups canned chicken broth and 2 cups water
     Pinch of dried chervil
     Salt and pepper to taste
½   cup light cream
2   Tbs. chopped parsley

1. Heat the butter in a heavy saucepan. Add the shallots and carrots. Cook, covered, over medium heat for about 10 minutes.

2. Sprinkle the flour over the carrots. Cook, stirring, for 2 minutes.

3. Stir in the hot stock and seasonings. Cook, partially covered, over low heat for 20 minutes.

4. Remove the solids from the soup and puree them in a blender or food processor. Return the puree to the liquid. (May be prepared ahead to this point.) Just before serving, add the cream and heat through without boiling. Garnish each serving with chopped parsley.

Gratin of Celery Root   SERVES 4

Celery root (knob celery or celeriac) is a winter vegetable in abundance from October through February. For some reason, it has been rather neglected in this country. This dish is an excellent way to serve celery root; its pronounced celery flavor comes right through.

2	pounds celery root, peeled Juice of one lemon		Salt and freshly ground black pepper to taste
1	small clove garlic Butter	½	cup light cream
		⅓	cup dry bread crumbs
½	cup grated Swiss cheese or a combination of Swiss and grated Parmesan cheese		

PREHEAT THE OVEN TO 375°.

1. Cut the celery root into ¼-inch-thick slices. Drop the slices into a large kettle and pour the lemon juice over them. Add enough cold water to cover and bring to a boil. Reduce the heat and simmer, uncovered, for 8 minutes. Drain well.

2. Rub a 10- or 12-inch oval casserole or gratin dish with the garlic (cut in half to release the juice). Butter the casserole well and place in it alternating layers of celery root and grated cheese. End with a layer of celery root. Add salt and pepper. Pour the cream over all. (May be prepared up to 2 hours ahead to this point and refrigerated; bring to room temperature before baking.)

3. Sprinkle the celery root with bread crumbs. Dot with butter and bake in a preheated 375° oven for 35 minutes. Serve hot, right from the casserole.

Herbed Wild Rice   SERVES 4

Wild rice is an expensive delicacy, but fortunately a small amount goes a long way. It is not a true rice, but the seed of a wild aquatic grass growing in lakes in the northern United States and Canada.

You'll notice the cooking time is quite a bit longer than for white rice. Be sure you've begun to simmer the rice about 20 minutes before you start to bake the gratin; the two should be ready together.

2	Tbs. butter	1¾	cups chicken stock (p. 207)
1	Tbs. minced shallots		or 1 cup canned chicken
1	Tbs. minced celery		broth and ¾ cup water
½	cup wild rice, rinsed in cold		*Bouquet garni* (1 sprig
	water		parsley, 1 bay leaf, ¼ tsp.
			dried thyme tied in
			cheesecloth)

1. Heat the butter in a 1½-quart saucepan. Add the onion and celery and cook over low heat until soft. Add the rice, stirring until well coated with butter.
2. Stir in the stock. Add the *bouquet garni.* Bring to a boil, stirring constantly. Reduce the heat and simmer, covered, for about 50 minutes or until the rice is tender.

Endive-Watercress Salad   SERVES 4

1	bunch watercress	1	tsp. Dijon mustard
3	heads Belgian endive	1	small clove garlic, crushed
1	Tbs. red wine vinegar		Freshly ground black pepper
¼	cup vegetable oil		

1. Trim the stems from the watercress. Cut the endive into thin lengthwise strips. Combine the greens in a large salad bowl.
2. Whisk the vinegar and oil together in a small bowl. Stir in the mustard, garlic, and black pepper to taste. Toss the salad with the dressing.

Oranges Grand Marnier SERVES 4

If you really want to pull out all the stops, serve the oranges with cool sabayon (p. 97) spooned over them.

4	Navel oranges	1	Tbs. Grand Marnier
½	cup fresh orange juice	½	tsp. sugar (or more,
1	Tbs. lemon juice		according to taste)

1. Peel the oranges. Remove as much of the white pith as possible. Cut into ¼-inch-thick slices.

2. Place the sliced oranges in a large shallow dish. Add the orange juice, lemon juice, and Grand Marnier. Sprinkle on the sugar. Cover and chill for at least 2 hours. Serve cold.

D I N N E R 22

ASPARAGUS with HERB MUSTARD SAUCE

VEGETABLE QUICHE JULIENNE

BRAISED BELGIAN ENDIVE

STEWED FRUIT COMPOTE

You've got an instant success on your hands with this sophisticated menu. One of the glories of quiche is the fact that it can be made in stages. This one tastes best eaten warm rather than hot, which means that as it "rests" you have ample time to prepare the braised Belgian endive. The first course and dessert may be made ahead of time and refrigerated.

Asparagus with Herb Mustard Sauce   SERVES 6

Fresh cold asparagus are accompanied by a piquant herbed mustard sauce.

36 **fresh, firm asparagus (about** **2½ to 3 pounds), peeled**	**1** **Tbs. each fresh minced** **parsley, chives, and shallots**
1 **cup mustard sauce (p. 110)**	

1. Trim the bottom of each asparagus, leaving a stalk about 5 or 6 inches long.
2. In a large skillet bring enough water to a boil to cover the asparagus when added. Add the asparagus and cover. Cook at a gentle boil for about

8 minutes or until crisp-tender (cooking time depends on size).

3. Drain immediately under cold running water. Refrigerate, covered, until serving time.

4. Make the mustard sauce (p. 110). Stir in the minced herbs and shallots. Refrigerate. To serve, arrange the asparagus spears on each of six plates; serve with the mustard sauce.

Vegetable Quiche Julienne   SERVES 6

Quiche—that unbeatable combination of tender, flaky crust and a savory custard filling. And it's all the more attractive for its ease of preparation.

4	Tbs. butter	4	large eggs
¾	cup celery, cut in julienne strips	1½	cups heavy cream
¾	cup leek (white part only), cut in julienne strips		One 9-inch partially baked tart shell (p. 203)
¾	cup green pepper, cut in julienne strips	¼	cup freshly grated Parmesan cheese
¾	cup carrot, cut in julienne strips	¼	cup freshly grated Gruyère cheese

PREHEAT THE OVEN TO 400°.

1. Heat the butter in a large heavy skillet. Add the vegetables and sauté over low heat for 3 minutes. Cover the pan and cook slowly for 10 minutes. Set aside.

2. In a large mixing bowl whisk together the eggs and cream. Stir in the vegetable mixture. (May be prepared ahead to this point and refrigerated.) Carefully pour the mixture into the partially baked tart shell. Place on a baking sheet and bake in a preheated 400° oven for 40 minutes. Sprinkle on the grated cheeses and bake 10 minutes longer. Allow the tart to rest at room temperature for half an hour before serving.

Braised Belgian Endive   SERVES 6

6	heads Belgian endive	½	cup water
2	Tbs. butter	1	Tbs. chopped parsley
1	Tbs. lemon juice		Salt and pepper to taste

1. Rinse the endives under running water. Pat dry with paper toweling.
2. Place the endives in a skillet in one layer with the butter, lemon juice, and water. Cover the pan and braise over low heat for 30 minutes. Check the pan from time to time to be sure the braising liquid does not evaporate completely; if necessary, add a tablespoon or two of water. Sprinkle with chopped parsley and salt and pepper. Serve hot.

Stewed Fruit Compote   SERVES 6

This iş a fine way to make use of dried fruit. The addition of lemon juice and cognac brings out the sweet-tart flavor of the fruit. If you cannot find dried cherries (usually available at specialty food shops), substitute dried peaches.

½	pound dried apricots	2	Tbs. lemon juice
½	pound dried apples	¾	cup sugar (or more to taste)
½	pound dried cherries, pitted	3	Tbs. cognac, optional
4	cups water		

Put the fruit in a saucepan with the water, lemon juice, and sugar. Bring to a boil. Reduce the heat and add the cognac if desired. Cover and simmer 15 minutes. Allow the fruit to cool in the syrup before chilling. Serve cold.

| D | I | N | N | E | R | | 23 |

FRESH MUSHROOM SOUP

SPINACH-STUFFED CRÊPES

GLAZED CARROTS (PP. 19-20)
or
BUTTERED SUGARSNAP PEAS

JERUSALEM ARTICHOKE SALAD

COLD ORANGE SABAYON

How pleasantly a bowl of warm soup gets this winter menu under way. With the exception of the vegetable accompaniment (carrots or peas), all the components of this menu may be prepared in advance.

Fresh Mushroom Soup   SERVES 4

Another silky soup, puréed to perfection, thanks to your tireless blender or food processor.

3	Tbs. butter	5	cups chicken stock (p. 207),
1/3	cup minced onions or shallots		heated, or 3 cups canned
1	pound mushrooms, coarsely		chicken broth and 2 cups
	chopped		water
2	Tbs. flour	1/4	cup heavy cream, optional
	Pinch of dried thyme	1	Tbs. minced parsley
	Salt and freshly ground black		
	pepper to taste		

1. Heat the butter in a medium-sized heavy saucepan. Add the onions and cook over low heat until soft.

2. Add the chopped mushrooms. Cook, stirring, for 5 minutes. Sprinkle the flour over the mushrooms, add the thyme and salt and pepper, and cook, stirring, for 3 minutes.

3. Gradually add the heated stock. Bring the soup to a boil, reduce the heat, and simmer, covered, for 30 minutes.

4. Remove the solids from the soup and puree in a blender or food processor. Return the puree to the soup. (May be prepared ahead to this point.) Just before serving, if desired, stir in the heavy cream and heat through without boiling. Garnish with chopped parsley.

Spinach-stuffed Crêpes   SERVES 4

Here is another delicious variation on the crêpe theme. This time the versatile pancakes hold a creamy filling of fresh spinach and cheese.

FOR THE CRÊPES:

Using the basic crêpe recipe on p. 203, prepare 12 7-inch crêpes. Cover with a damp cloth and set aside.

FOR THE SPINACH-CHEESE FILLING:

2½	pounds spinach, rinsed, tough stems removed	¾	cup freshly grated Parmesan cheese
3	Tbs. butter	2	eggs
2	Tbs. chopped onions or shallots		Salt and pepper to taste
½	cup grated Gruyère cheese	3	Tbs. butter, softened to room temperature
			Extra Parmesan cheese

1. Plunge the spinach into a large kettle of boiling water. Cook, covered, until the spinach wilts. Drain immediately in a colander under cold running water. Wring the spinach in a kitchen towel to remove excess moisture.

2. Heat the butter in a skillet. Add the onions and cook until soft. Add the spinach and cook, stirring, for a few minutes until the spinach is dry. Let cool slightly.

3. Put the spinach in a blender or food processor with the Gruyère, Parmesan, eggs, and salt and pepper. Process until smooth. (May be prepared ahead to this point and refrigerated; bring filling to room temperature before proceeding.)

PREHEAT THE OVEN TO 400°.

4. Place a small amount of filling in each crêpe. Roll to enclose the filling and place seam side down in a buttered baking dish. Brush the crêpes with softened butter and sprinkle with extra Parmesan cheese. Bake in a preheated 400° oven for 15 minutes or until the crêpes are lightly browned.

Buttered Sugarsnap Peas   SERVES 4

Sugarsnap peas resemble sweet peas, but they have smaller greener pods that are edible. They should be cooked quickly and simply to preserve their flavor and texture.

1¼	pounds sugarsnap pea pods	2	Tbs. butter, softened

1. Trim the pea pods at both ends and remove any strings.

2. Cook the pods in boiling water to cover for 2 minutes. Drain well. Add softened butter and serve hot in a warmed vegetable dish.

Jerusalem Artichoke Salad   SERVES 4

The Jerusalem artichoke is not an artichoke at all. It's a tuber or root vegetable belonging to the sunflower family. Its flavor, which is mild and nutlike, vaguely resembles the globe artichoke. Jerusalem artichokes are readily available all winter long; they are sometimes called sunchokes.

¾ pound Jerusalem artichokes, peeled and sliced thin	1 clove garlic, crushed
1 Tbs. lemon juice	1 tsp. Dijon mustard
¼ cup vegetable oil	Lettuce leaves

1. Put the sliced Jerusalem artichokes in a salad bowl.
2. Whisk together the lemon juice and vegetable oil. Add the garlic and mustard. Pour the dressing over the Jerusalem artichokes. Cover and chill for at least 2 hours. Divide the salad among 4 plates lined with lettuce leaves.

Cold Orange Sabayon   SERVES 4

This airy custard is a relative of the Italian dessert zabaglione. It does not require last-minute preparation because it is served cold. Cold orange sabayon may also be served as a sauce over fresh fruit or berries.

4 egg yolks	¼ cup heavy cream, stiffly beaten
½ cup sugar	
⅓ cup orange liqueur (Grand Marnier or Cointreau)	

1. Combine the egg yolks, sugar, and liqueur in the top half of a double boiler. Whisk the mixture continuously over simmering water until thickened, about 8 to 10 minutes.
2. Place the top half of the double boiler over a bowl of cracked ice and continue to beat until the sauce has cooled.
3. Fold in the stiffly beaten cream and divide the sabayon among 4 long-stemmed glasses. Refrigerate.

CHINESE SESAME NOODLES

HOT-and-SPICY BRAISED EGGPLANT (PP. 26-27)

ASPARAGUS and BEAN SPROUT SALAD

ALMOND COOKIES

Here is a Chinese meal that needs no last-minute preparation. This menu would be a good choice for a late supper or a picnic with friends. Everything can be made ahead. If it's to be a picnic, carry along fresh fruit in season for dessert.

Chinese Sesame Noodles   SERVES 4

This is an excellent recipe for an oriental pasta salad. I am very grateful to Phillipe Berard, the chef and owner of Self Chef in New York City, for sharing it with me.

1	Tbs. chunky-style peanut butter	1	tsp. minced garlic
¼	cup soy sauce	2	ounces snow peas, cut in julienne strips
¼	cup oriental sesame oil	½	pound very thin Chinese egg noodles (available in oriental markets)
½	cup peanut oil		
1	Tbs. oriental hot oil (available in oriental markets)		
1	tsp. minced fresh ginger	2	Tbs. toasted sesame seeds
		2	scallions, including green tops, chopped

1. In a mixing bowl whisk together the peanut butter, soy sauce, oils, ginger, and garlic. Set the dressing aside.

2. Blanch the snow peas in boiling water to cover for 30 seconds. Drain and refresh under cold running water. Set aside.

3. Drop the noodles into 4 quarts of rapidly boiling water. Cook, stirring to separate the strands, for 2 minutes after the water returns to a boil. Do not overcook. Drain in a colander.

3. While the noodles are still warm, pour on the dressing. Add the sesame seeds, scallions, and blanched snow peas. Toss well. Refrigerate. Serve cold or at room temperature.

Asparagus and Bean Sprout Salad   SERVES 4

½	pound very thin asparagus, peeled and cut into 1-inch lengths	2	Tbs. peanut oil
		1	Tbs. oriental sesame oil
		1	Tbs. peeled shredded ginger root
¾	pound bean sprouts		
2	Tbs. rice wine vinegar	1	clove garlic, crushed
3	Tbs. soy sauce		

1. Cook the asparagus in boiling water to cover for 30 seconds. Drain immediately under cold running water. Set aside.

2. Put the bean sprouts in a colander and pour 2 quarts of boiling water over them. Pat dry with paper toweling. Combine the bean sprouts and asparagus in a large mixing bowl.

3. In a small bowl whisk together the vinegar, soy sauce, and oils. Stir in the ginger and garlic. Pour the dressing over the vegetables and toss well. Refrigerate.

Almond Cookies

These are not the almond cookies one usually finds in Chinese restaurants, but I think you'll agree they're good. This recipe makes about 6 dozen cookies, which will probably disappear at once. If there are any left over, you may keep them a week in a loosely sealed container in a cool dry place.

2	**large eggs, at room temperature**	**½**	**tsp. vanilla**
½	**cup sugar**	**⅔**	**cup all-purpose flour, sifted**
		¼	**cup blanched sliced almonds**

PREHEAT THE OVEN TO 400°.

1. Line 2 baking sheets (approximately 18″ × 12″) with parchment. Set aside.

2. Combine the eggs, sugar, and vanilla in the bowl of an electric mixer. Beat at high speed until the mixture is pale yellow and forms a thick ribbon, about 5 minutes.

3. Gently but thoroughly fold in the sifted flour. Do not overfold. Fit a pastry bag with a no. 6 plain tube and fill it with the mixture. Pipe 1-inch-long cookies onto the prepared sheets. Leave ¾ inch between cookies. Sprinkle the almonds over the cookies and bake in a preheated 400° oven for 10 minutes or until the cookies are lightly browned. Remove immediately and let cool. The cookies will become crisp in a matter of minutes, and you'll be able to remove them easily from the parchment.

CREAM of CAULIFLOWER SOUP (PP. 18-19)
or
EGGPLANT CAVIAR

WINE-BRAISED VEGETABLE STEW

HERBED RICE

APRICOT SOUFFLÉS

A well-rounded autumn repast begins with a choice of cream of cauliflower soup or eggplant caviar. If you choose the eggplant appetizer, plan to prepare it a day in advance.

Eggplant Caviar   SERVES 4

Garlic-infused, silky eggplant caviar is a very satisfying appetizer. It's good with drinks, too, as an hors d'oeuvre spread on freshly made croutons.

2 medium-sized eggplants	1 Tbs. lemon juice
3 large cloves garlic, crushed	1/4 tsp. Dijon mustard
1 egg yolk	Salt and pepper to taste
1/3 cup oil (combine olive oil and vegetable oil)	4 lettuce leaves
	1 Tbs. minced fresh parsley

PREHEAT THE OVEN TO 400°.

1. Pierce the eggplants with a fork in several places. Place on a baking sheet and bake in a preheated 400° oven for 40 to 50 minutes or until soft to the touch. When cool enough to handle, split the eggplants in half and scoop out the pulp.

2. In a mixing bowl mash together the eggplant and garlic. Using a wooden mallet, puree the eggplant by pushing it through a fine sieve into a bowl. You may use the food processor or blender for this, but the texture of the puree will not be as smooth.

3. Add the egg yolk to the puree and whisk in the oil by drops as if making mayonnaise. Stir in the lemon juice and mustard, salt and pepper. Refrigerate. Serve the eggplant on lettuce leaves garnished with chopped parsley.

Wine-braised Vegetable Stew   SERVES 4

The success of this dish depends on accurate timing. The vegetables are cooked in stages to insure their crispness. The total cooking time for this savory stew is about half an hour; blanching, peeling, and cutting tasks may be done hours before the final cooking.

2	cups broccoli flowerets	3	parsley sprigs
1	cup cauliflower flowerets	¼	pound small white onions,
½	cup olive oil		peeled
½	pound small mushrooms,	2	cups water
	stems trimmed	2	Tbs. tomato paste
½	pound finger carrots, peeled	1	large red bell pepper, seeded,
1	tsp. minced garlic		cut into ¼-inch strips
1	cup dry white wine	1	small zucchini, cut into 1-inch
1	bay leaf		cubes
¼	tsp. dried thyme		

1. Blanch the broccoli and cauliflower in boiling water to cover for 2 minutes. Drain under cold running water. Pat dry and set aside.

2. Heat the olive oil in a large heavy casserole. When it is quite hot, add the mushrooms and carrots; sauté 1 minute. Add the garlic and sauté, stirring 1 minute more.

3. Add the wine and herbs. Cook over high heat until the liquid is reduced to about ½ cup.

4. Add the onions, water, and tomato paste. Cook over high heat until the onions are just tender, about 8 or 9 minutes. Add the red pepper, zucchini, and the reserved broccoli and cauliflower. Cook, covered, over moderate heat for 4 minutes. Serve the stew piping hot.

Herbed Rice   SERVES 4

2	Tbs. butter	½	cup canned chicken broth
2	Tbs. chopped onion	1	bay leaf
1	cup rice	¼	tsp. thyme
1	cup water		Salt and pepper to taste

1. Heat the butter in a heavy saucepan. Add the onion and cook until soft. Add the rice and stir until well coated with butter.

2. Add the water, chicken broth, bay leaf, thyme, and salt and pepper. Bring to a boil. Cover and simmer for 18 minutes. The rice may be kept warm, tightly covered, for 10 to 15 minutes. Fluff with a fork before serving.

Apricot Soufflés   SERVES 4

Four individual, ethereal soufflés—a perfectly marvelous finale. These soufflés can be prepared and baked in 20 minutes, making this a very easy last-minute dessert. Your guests will be more than appreciative.

1	Tbs. softened butter	1	tsp. grated orange peel
	Sugar	2	Tbs. apricot liqueur
3	egg yolks	3	egg whites
⅓	cup plus 2 Tbs. sugar		Confectioners' sugar
¼	cup apricot preserves		

PREHEAT THE OVEN TO 450°.

1. Butter the bottom and sides of 4 ¾-cup soufflé molds. Sprinkle the insides lightly with sugar.

2. In a mixing bowl beat together the egg yolks and ⅓ cup sugar until the mixture is pale yellow and forms a ribbon. Stir in the preserves, orange peel, and liqueur.

3. Beat the egg whites until they hold soft peaks; gradually add 2 tablespoons sugar and continue beating until the egg whites are stiff and shiny.

4. Gently fold the egg whites into the apricot mixture. Spoon the mixture evenly into each soufflé dish. Place the soufflés on a baking sheet and bake in a preheated 450° oven for 12 to 14 minutes. Serve immediately, dusted with confectioners' sugar.

ROASTED PEPPERS

WHOLE WHEAT GARLIC BREAD

PASTA with BROCCOLI SAUCE

FRESH MUSHROOM SALAD

TORTONI

An informal Italian menu that you can put together in any season. Plump roasted peppers bathed in olive oil may be prepared a day in advance; so may the tortoni.

Roasted Peppers   SERVES 4

6	large red or green bell peppers	½	cup olive oil
2	tsp. red wine vinegar	1	clove garlic, crushed
		1	tsp. dried oregano

PREHEAT THE BROILER.

1. Place the peppers on the broiler rack close to the flame. Broil, turning the peppers from time to time, until their skins are charred all over.

2. Remove from the broiler. When the peppers are cool enough to handle, peel them.

3. Cut the peppers in half lengthwise; remove the seeds and pulp. Pat dry with paper toweling.

4. Place the peppers in a flat dish; sprinkle with vinegar. Add the olive oil, garlic, and oregano. Refrigerate several hours or overnight. Bring to room temperature before serving.

Whole Wheat Garlic Bread   SERVES 4

Buy a good, crusty, freshly baked Italian bread for this.

1	loaf Italian whole wheat bread	¼	tsp. dried oregano, crushed
⅓	cup olive oil		Freshly ground black pepper
1	clove garlic, finely minced		

PREHEAT THE OVEN TO 350°.

1. Cut the bread in half lengthwise.

2. Combine the olive oil, garlic, and oregano. Brush the cut sides of the bread liberally with the flavored oil.

3. Wrap the bread in foil and bake in a preheated 350° oven for 15 minutes. Cut the bread into crosswise sections and serve hot.

Pasta with Broccoli Sauce   SERVES 4

The approach of this recipe reflects the new attitude toward pasta sauces—it is very uncomplicated. The pasta retains its own identity because it's not drowning in a heavy sea of sauce.

2	cups broccoli flowerets, about 1 inch long	2	Tbs. softened butter
½	cup olive oil	½	cup freshly grated Parmesan cheese
2	tsp. minced garlic		Freshly ground black pepper to taste
1	pound thin spaghetti or thin linguine		

1. Cook the broccoli flowerets in boiling water to cover for 1 minute. They should be crisp-tender. Drain and reserve.

2. Heat the olive oil in a medium saucepan. Add the minced garlic and cook over low heat until the garlic has barely colored. Remove from the heat.

3. Cook the pasta in 5 quarts of rapidly boiling water until *al dente* (firm to the bite; do not overcook). While the pasta is cooking, put the reserved broccoli in the pan with the garlic and oil and heat through for a minute or two.

4. Drain the pasta and place it in a warmed serving dish. Add the butter, toss well, and pour on the broccoli sauce. Sprinkle with Parmesan and toss again. Serve immediately with freshly ground pepper.

Fresh Mushroom Salad   SERVES 4

1	pound firm, unblemished mushrooms, stems trimmed	2	Tbs. minced parsley
1	clove garlic, peeled	¹/₃	cup olive oil
	Juice of 1 small lemon		Salt and freshly ground black pepper to taste

Slice the mushrooms thin. Rub the inside of a bowl with garlic; add the mushrooms. Toss with lemon juice, parsley, and olive oil. Just before serving, add the salt and pepper.

Tortoni   SERVES 4

A creamy, Marsala-laced frozen dessert that takes just minutes to make.

1	cup heavy cream	2	Tbs. dry Marsala
2	Tbs. confectioners' sugar	1	egg white at room temperature, stiffly beaten
2	Tbs. crushed amaretti (Italian macaroons)		

1. Whip the cream in a well-chilled bowl using chilled beaters or a whisk until the cream forms soft peaks.

2. Gently fold in the sugar, macaroons, and Marsala.

3. Fold in the egg white. Turn the mixture into 4 individual half-cup ramekins. Freeze for at least 2 hours. Let stand at room temperature for 10 minutes before serving. Covered tightly with plastic wrap, tortoni may be kept frozen for up to 3 weeks.

ARTICHOKES with MUSTARD SAUCE

CHEESE SOUFFLÉ

SHREDDED SAUTÉED ZUCCHINI

APPLE STREUSEL

You can assemble this menu whenever the mood strikes you; the ingredients are available year round.

Artichokes with Mustard Sauce   SERVES 4

A classic (make-ahead) appetizer that brings an air of elegance to any meal.

4	medium to large artichokes	4	quarts water
	Acidulated water (1 Tbs.	2	Tbs. lemon juice
	lemon juice in a quart of	1	Tbs. olive oil
	water)		

1. To prepare the artichokes for cooking, cut off the stems almost flush with the base so they'll stand upright when served. Remove several layers of tough outer leaves all the way around the base.
2. With a very sharp knife cut off the top third of the artichoke or use

scissors to cut off the spiked part of each leaf. Once the cut surfaces are exposed to air, artichokes discolor rapidly. To prevent this, have acidulated water ready and drop the artichokes into it as soon as you've cut them.

3. Use a nonaluminum pot. Bring to a boil 4 quarts of water to which you have added 2 tablespoons lemon juice and 1 tablespoon olive oil. Cook the artichokes, covered, at a slow boil for 40 minutes or until tender. Test by removing an outer leaf; it should pull away easily.

4. Turn the artichokes upside down on a large platter to drain. When cool enough to handle, carefully remove the fuzzy "choke" in the center of each artichoke. I find a small pointed grapefruit spoon ideal for this job, or you can use a melon-ball cutter. Serve the artichokes at room temperature and fill the center of each with mustard sauce.

Mustard Sauce   Makes about 1 cup

3	Tbs. Dijon mustard	½	cup vegetable oil
	Scant ¼ cup boiling water	1	tsp. lemon juice

Put the mustard in the container of a blender or food processor fitted with the metal blade. With the machine running, add the water in a thin stream, then slowly add the oil by drops as if for mayonnaise. Turn the sauce into a bowl and stir in the lemon juice. Refrigerate.

Cheese Soufflé   SERVES 4

Everyone is dazzled by the magic of a soufflé. You may prepare this dish in stages if you like; cook the cheese-flavored sauce base and set it aside until you are ready to incorporate the egg whites. Slip the soufflé into the oven just before serving the artichokes.

3	Tbs. butter	¾	cup grated Swiss cheese or a
3	Tbs. flour		combination of Swiss and
1	cup boiling milk		grated Parmesan cheese
4	egg yolks, at room		Salt and pepper to taste
	temperature		Pinch of nutmeg
		4	egg whites, at room
			temperature, stiffly beaten

1. Melt the butter in a heavy saucepan. Add the flour; cook, stirring, over medium heat for 2 minutes; do not let the flour brown. Pour in the boiling milk and beat over medium heat until very thick.

PREHEAT THE OVEN TO 375°.

2. Away from the heat, beat in the egg yolks one at a time. Stir in the cheese, salt and pepper, and nutmeg. The sauce base should be very smooth. (May be prepared ahead to this point. Before proceeding with the recipe, reheat the sauce to tepid.)

3. Stir about one-quarter of the beaten egg whites into the soufflé mixture to lighten it. Gently fold in the remaining egg whites. Turn the mixture into a well-buttered 1½-quart soufflé case. Bake in a preheated 375° oven for 25 to 30 minutes or until the soufflé is puffed and evenly browned. Serve immediately.

Shredded Sautéed Zucchini   SERVES 4

There seems to be no end to the ways in which one can prepare zucchini. This is a particularly good dish that takes only minutes to cook.

1½	pounds zucchini	1	Tbs. butter
	Salt	2	Tbs. chopped scallions
2	Tbs. olive oil		

1. Grate and salt the zucchini as for zucchini fritters (p. 77). Wring in a kitchen towel to remove excess moisture.

2. Heat the oil and butter in a large heavy skillet. Stir in the scallions and cook briefly—do not brown.

3. Add the shredded zucchini and cook over moderate heat, stirring and tossing, until the zucchini is heated through, about 3 or 4 minutes.

4. Turn into a warmed, buttered vegetable dish and serve immediately.

Apple Streusel   SERVES 4

There's nothing like a cinnamon-studded apple dessert to bring back memories of childhood—even if your mother never heard of it! The nostalgia is in the taste and texture of the dessert itself.

1½ **pounds Golden Delicious apples, peeled and sliced (about 4 cups) Lemon juice**	**Pinch of nutmeg**
⅓ **cup sugar**	¼ **tsp. ground cinnamon**
⅓ **cup brown sugar**	¾ **cup flour**
	4 **ounces butter, in small pieces**
	Heavy cream (optional)

PREHEAT THE OVEN TO 350°.

1. Sprinkle the sliced apples with lemon juice and pile them into a buttered 8-inch pie plate with deep sides. Set aside while preparing the streusel.

2. Place the dry ingredients and butter in a food processor or blender. Process until the mixture resembles coarse meal.

3. Sprinkle the streusel thickly over the apples and bake, covered, in a 350° oven for 20 minutes. Uncover and bake 30 minutes more or until the streusel is crisp and lightly browned. Serve warm or cold with heavy cream if desired.

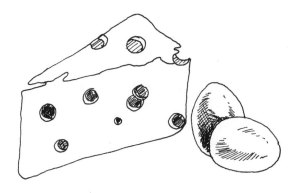

FRESH TOMATO BASIL SOUP (PP. 76-77)

STUFFED PEPPERS NIÇOISE

HERBED RICE (P. 103)

GREEN BEANS VINAIGRETTE

PEACHES with FRESH RASPBERRY SAUCE

Celebrate summer's bounty with a dinner full of garden freshness—and prepare almost all of it ahead. Plan to serve the tomato basil soup cold, leaving just the rice to be readied at serving time.

Stuffed Peppers Niçoise   SERVES 4

4	medium-sized bell peppers (2 red, 2 green)	1	pound tomatoes, peeled, seeded, and chopped
1	eggplant, about 1½ pounds, cubed	¼	cup pitted oil-cured olives, chopped
	Salt	2	Tbs. pine nuts
3	Tbs. olive oil	2	Tbs. chopped parsley
1	medium onion, chopped	1	tsp. dried basil
1	clove garlic, minced	½	tsp. dried oregano

1. Cut the peppers in half lengthwise, removing the tops, seeds, and white pulp. Set aside.

2. Sprinkle the cubed eggplant with salt and place in a colander with a weight on it (a heavy pot will do). Let it drain this way for 40 minutes. Dry the eggplant with paper toweling.

PREHEAT THE OVEN TO 375°.

3. Heat the olive oil in a large heavy skillet. Sauté the eggplant until tender and lightly browned. Remove to a bowl with a slotted spoon.

4. To the oil remaining in the pan add the onion and cook until soft. Add the garlic and tomatoes and cook over high heat until the tomato juices are almost evaporated.

5. Combine the tomato mixture with the reserved eggplant and add the remaining ingredients. Mix well and divide the mixture evenly among the pepper halves. (May be prepared ahead to this point.)

6. Arrange the peppers in an oiled baking dish. Bake in a preheated 375° oven for 45 minutes. Offer two halves to each guest and serve with herbed rice.

Green Beans Vinaigrette   SERVES 4

The beans emerge from their brief cooking very green and very crisp. To retain that beautiful color, add the dressing only at the moment of serving.

1	pound green beans, cut into 1½-inch lengths	1	tsp. dried basil Salt and pepper to taste
1	Tbs. red wine vinegar	1	Tbs. finely chopped shallots
4	Tbs. olive oil		

1. Cook the beans in rapidly boiling water to cover for 40 seconds. Drain immediately under cold running water. Refrigerate, tightly covered.

2. In a small bowl whisk together the vinegar and oil. Add the basil and salt and pepper. Just before serving, sprinkle the beans with shallots and toss with vinaigrette.

Peaches with Fresh Raspberry Sauce   SERVES 4

Nothing says summer better than sweet sun-ripened peaches and fresh raspberries.

4	large ripe peaches, peeled	1	Tbs. superfine sugar (or
2	Tbs. lemon juice		more, to taste)
1½	cups fresh raspberries		

1. Plunge the peaches into boiling water for 30 seconds to facilitate peeling.

2. Slice the peaches and arrange them in a serving dish. Sprinkle with lemon juice to prevent discoloration. Refrigerate, covered.

3. Make the raspberry sauce. Place the raspberries and sugar in the container of a food processor or blender. Puree the mixture until the sugar dissolves. Rub the puree through a sieve to remove the seeds. Chill. Arrange the sliced peaches on each of 4 plates and spoon on the raspberry sauce.

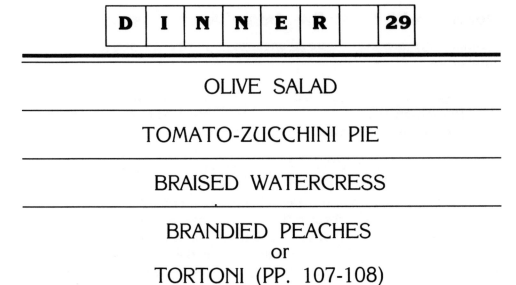

DINNER 29

OLIVE SALAD

TOMATO-ZUCCHINI PIE

BRAISED WATERCRESS

BRANDIED PEACHES
or
TORTONI (PP. 107-108)

Depending on your choice of dessert, this menu could be either summer or winter fare. Both desserts are of the make-ahead variety, and so is the olive salad. The tomato-zucchini pie may be made in stages to suit your convenience. Prepare braised watercress (5 minutes) at serving time.

Olive Salad   SERVES 4

1/3 pound imported Swiss cheese, cut into julienne strips	1 1/4 cups small pimiento-stuffed green olives
1/4 cup chopped scallions, including green tops	Freshly ground black pepper to taste
2 stalks celery, sliced thin	1 Tbs. lemon juice
	4 Tbs. olive oil
	Boston lettuce leaves

1. Combine the first 5 ingredients in a large mixing bowl.

2. Whisk together the lemon juice and olive oil. Just before serving, pour the dressing over the salad and toss gently. Serve on plates lined with Boston lettuce.

Tomato-Zucchini Pie   SERVES 4

If you want to make this pie in winter, use canned Italian tomatoes. Winter tomatoes are expensive and tasteless.

2	Tbs. olive oil	2	Tbs. chopped parsley
¾	cup chopped onion	¼	tsp. dried basil
1	pound can Italian tomatoes, drained and coarsely chopped, or		Pinch of dried marjoram Salt and pepper to taste
1	pound fresh tomatoes, peeled, seeded, and chopped	2	eggs, well beaten
1	large clove garlic, chopped	1	partially baked 9-inch tart shell (p. 203)
½	pound zucchini, sliced thin	¼	cup freshly grated Parmesan cheese

PREHEAT THE OVEN TO 400°.

1. Heat the olive oil in a large heavy skillet. Add the onion and sauté until soft.

2. Add the tomato, garlic, and zucchini. Stir in the herbs and salt and pepper. Simmer the mixture, uncovered, for 12 minutes. Cool slightly. (Filling may be prepared ahead to this point.)

3. Combine the eggs and tomato-zucchini mixture; turn into the partially baked tart shell. Sprinkle with Parmesan cheese. Bake the pie in a preheated 400° oven for 20 minutes. Serve hot.

Braised Watercress   SERVES 4

3   bunches watercress,   2   Tbs. chicken stock or canned
      untrimmed   chicken broth
¼   cup butter

1. Wash the watercress well but do not pat it dry.
2. Melt the butter in a large saucepan. Add the watercress and cook, covered, until wilted.
3. Add the chicken stock, uncover the pan, and cook until most of the liquid has evaporated. Serve hot.

Brandied Peaches   SERVES 4

Perfectly poached fresh peaches in brandy syrup—a very special way to end a good dinner.

1¼   cups sugar   ⅓   cup brandy
2½   cups water   ⅛   tsp. vanilla
4   large, firm, ripe peaches

1. Make poaching syrup. Combine the sugar and water in an enameled saucepan. Bring to a boil. Reduce the heat and simmer, covered, for 15 minutes.
2. Poach the peaches in the syrup for 12 minutes or until barely tender. Allow the peaches to cool in the syrup. Remove to a bowl.
3. Add the brandy and vanilla to the syrup. Cook over medium heat for 5 minutes. Peel the peaches, pour on the syrup, and chill well. Serve in long-stemmed glasses with a spoonful or two of brandy syrup.

CAPONATA

SPINACH FETTUCCINE with MUSHROOM SAUCE

SWISS CHARD, ITALIAN STYLE

ALMOND TART
or
PEARS with GORGONZOLA

What could be a more fitting prelude to an Italian dinner than caponata, that celebrated eggplant appetizer? If you want to make this an "anytime of the year" menu, substitute spinach for the Swiss chard, which is available only from May through September.

Caponata   SERVES 6

A small amount of vinegar gives caponata its characteristic "pickled" flavor (indeed, caponata is frequently called pickled eggplant). It tastes even better the second day.

1	eggplant, about 1¼ pounds	1	Tbs. tomato paste
	Salt	2	Tbs. red wine vinegar
⅓	cup olive oil	1	cup small pitted green olives
½	cup chopped onion	1	tsp. sugar
1	cup diced celery	¼	tsp. hot dried pepper flakes
1	cup fresh tomato, cubed, or 1 cup Italian plum tomatoes, drained and chopped		

1. Do not peel the eggplant. Cut it into 1-inch cubes. Sprinkle the cubes with salt and place in a colander, weighted (a heavy pot will do). Let it drain this way for 40 minutes. Dry the eggplant between pieces of paper toweling.

2. Heat the oil in a large heavy skillet; when it is very hot, add the eggplant (you may have to do this in two batches). Cook, stirring and tossing, until well browned on all sides. Remove to a bowl using a slotted spoon.

3. To the oil remaining in the skillet add the onion and celery. Cook, stirring, until the onion is soft. Add the tomato, cover, and cook over low heat for 5 minutes.

4. Add the remaining ingredients and the reserved eggplant. Blend well and cover. Cook over low heat for 5 minutes longer. Cool the mixture before refrigerating. Serve chilled or at room temperature with a good fresh Italian bread.

Spinach Fettuccine with Mushroom Sauce   SERVES 6

If you have a source for homemade fettuccine noodles, try them in this dish.

Mushroom sauce (see p. 64)
1¼ pounds spinach fettuccine

Freshly grated Parmesan cheese

1. Prepare the mushroom sauce according to the directions in the recipe for Swiss crêpes with mushroom sauce. Keep warm, covered.

2. Cook the fettuccine in a large quantity of rapidly boiling water until it is *al dente* (firm to the bite; do not overcook). Drain well. Place the fettuccine in a large, warmed, deep serving dish. Spoon on the mushroom sauce, toss well, and serve immediately with freshly grated Parmesan cheese.

Swiss Chard, Italian Style   SERVES 6

Swiss chard has a subtle, barely sweet flavor that somewhat resembles spinach. The two are frequently used interchangeably. Its greenish-white stalks are edible, retaining their crunchy texture when cooked along with the leaves.

2	pounds Swiss chard	2	Tbs. freshly grated Parmesan cheese
1	Tbs. lemon juice		Salt and freshly ground black pepper
4	Tbs. olive oil		

1. Cut the chard (including stems) into bite-sized pieces. Rinse well under running water.

2. Cook the chard in rapidly boiling water to cover for 5 minutes or until just tender. Drain in a colander and squeeze out as much water as possible. Remove to a bowl.

3. Whisk together the lemon juice and olive oil. Pour over the warm chard, sprinkle with grated cheese, and toss well. Add salt and freshly ground black pepper to taste. Serve warm or at room temperature.

Note: If Swiss chard is not available, substitute fresh spinach and cook just until wilted; proceed with the recipe. Plan to serve the spinach warm.

Almond Tart   SERVES 6

1	recipe pâte brisée sucrée (p. 203) Almond cream (frangipane), pp. 23-24	½	cup blanched sliced or slivered almonds Apricot glaze (p. 206)

1. Roll the dough out to a thickness of ⅛ inch. Fit it into a 9-inch tart pan with removable ring. Let rest in the refrigerator for at least 2 hours.

2. Prick the bottom of the tart shell all over with a fork. Spread the almond cream evenly over the bottom of the shell and sprinkle on the sliced almonds. Bake the tart in a preheated 400° oven for 45 to 50 minutes. Remove from the oven and brush with apricot glaze. Serve at room temperature.

Pears with Gorgonzola   SERVES 6

An alternate way to end the meal is with one of Italy's best-loved desserts—
sweet ripe pears with creamy Gorgonzola cheese.

3   ripe pears, halved
**6   ounces Gorgonzola cheese,
       softened**

1. Use a melon ball cutter to core the pear halves.
2. Mash the cheese with a fork until it is smooth. Spoon equal amounts of
cheese into the cavity of each pear, mounding it slightly. Refrigerate. Let
stand at room temperature for 15 minutes before serving.

COLD CREAM of CAULIFLOWER SOUP
(PP. 18-19)

CRÊPES with TOMATO MOUSSE

SORREL PUREE

STRAWBERRIES with STRAWBERRY SAUCE

Here is an attractive summer meal, much of which may be prepared ahead. Since you'll want the soup very cold, make it a day ahead and keep refrigerated. The dessert also could be readied the day before. The tomatoes for the tomato mousse can be simmering while the crêpe batter "rests." At serving time assemble the crêpes and heat through in a moderately hot oven; make the sorrel puree (7 minutes).

Crêpes with Tomato Mousse   SERVES 4

With the addition of stiffly beaten egg whites, a tomato puree becomes a mousse with just enough body to be wrapped in a crêpe. You may serve the sorrel puree either as a sauce, over the crêpes, or as a vegetable accompaniment.

FOR THE CRÊPES:

Using the basic crêpe recipe on p. 203, prepare 12 6-inch crêpes. Cover with a damp cloth and set aside.

FOR THE TOMATO MOUSSE:

2 Tbs. butter	1 Tbs. tomato paste
2 Tbs. chopped shallots or onions	3 egg whites, stiffly beaten
3 pounds ripe plum tomatoes, peeled, seeded, and chopped	Butter

1. Melt the butter in a large heavy saucepan. Add the shallots or onions and cook until soft. Add the tomatoes and tomato paste. Cook, uncovered, over low heat for about 1 hour or until the mixture is reduced to a puree and most of the moisture has evaporated. The tomato puree must be cool before you add the beaten egg whites. To hasten cooling, stir the purée in a bowl over ice.

PREHEAT THE OVEN TO 400°.

2. Just before you are ready to stuff the crêpes, fold the beaten egg whites into the tomato puree. Place about 2 tablespoons of tomato mousse in each crêpe. Roll them and arrange them seam side down in a buttered baking dish; dot with butter. Bake in a preheated 400° oven for 15 minutes or until the crêpes are golden brown. Serve hot.

Sorrel Puree   SERVES 4

Sorrel is one of the easiest vegetables to prepare. In practically no time at all, it reduces to a puree as it cooks.

1½ pounds sorrel, stems removed	Salt and pepper to taste
3 Tbs. butter	

1. Cut the sorrel leaves into lengthwise shreds (*chiffonade*). Rinse under running water and shake dry.

2. Melt the butter in a heavy saucepan. Stir in the sorrel and cook, covered, over low heat about 7 minutes. Season with salt and pepper to taste. For a very smooth puree, rub the sorrel through a fine sieve. Reheat gently before serving.

Strawberries with Strawberry Sauce SERVES 4

1½	pints strawberries, rinsed and hulled	1	tsp. lemon juice
		2	Tbs. granulated brown sugar

1. Reserve half a pint of berries for the strawberry sauce. If the remaining berries are very large, cut them in half lengthwise; otherwise, leave whole. Refrigerate, covered.

2. Make the strawberry sauce. Puree the reserved strawberries in a food processor or blender. Add the lemon juice. Chill. To serve, arrange the strawberries on each of 4 plates. Spoon on the sauce and sprinkle each serving with brown sugar.

D I N N E R 32

TAPENADE with CRUDITÉS
or
PEPERONATA

SPINACH GNOCCHI

JERUSALEM ARTICHOKE SALAD (P. 97)

WARM APPLE FRITTERS

This is the sort of dinner that ideally should be eaten with family or friends in the kitchen. That way you'll be able to serve the gnocchi gloriously hot from the oven and eat the apple fritters hot out of the frying pan. Both first courses and the Jerusalem artichoke salad may be prepared ahead. Tapenade with crudités is especially easy since there's no cooking involved.

Tapenade with Crudités   SERVES 4

A fragrant blend of olives, anchovies, tuna, and garlic—that's tapenade. Along the Mediterranean everyone eats *pain bagnat,* crusty French bread spread with this Provençal mixture. Use it as a filling for hollowed-out tomatoes or halved avocados.

½ pound black Italian or Greek olives, pitted	3½ ounce can imported Italian tuna in olive oil
4 flat anchovy fillets	3 Tbs. olive oil
1½ Tbs. capers	Freshly ground black pepper
2 cloves garlic	

1. Put the olives, anchovies, capers, garlic, and tuna, including the oil in which it is packed, in the container of a food processor or blender. Purée the mixture.

2. With the motor running, slowly add the olive oil. Blend well. Remove to a bowl and season with pepper to taste. Arrange a selection of any of the following fresh vegetables on a platter: broccoli flowerets, red or green bell peppers cut into strips, celery sticks, carrot sticks, radishes, scallions, zucchini slices, snow peas. Serve with the tapenade.

Peperonata   SERVES 4

A good Italian appetizer combining bell peppers with tomato, onion, and a hint of garlic.

4 medium red or green bell peppers, seeds and pith removed	3 large ripe tomatoes, peeled and seeded, or use canned tomatoes, drained
3 Tbs. olive oil	Freshly ground black pepper
1 medium onion, sliced	
1 large clove garlic, chopped	

1. Cut the peppers into thick strips. Set aside.

2. Heat the olive oil in a heavy skillet. Add the onion and garlic and sauté over low heat for 2 or 3 minutes.

3. Add the peppers to the skillet. Cut the tomatoes in half and lay them over the peppers. Sprinkle with black pepper to taste. Cover and cook over low heat for 10 minutes. Remove the cover and cook 10 minutes more or until the peppers are tender but not mushy. Serve hot or at room temperature.

Spinach Gnocchi   SERVES 4

These are tiny dumplings of spinach and ricotta cheese briefly heated in butter and Parmesan cheese—a rich and delicious main course.

2	Tbs. butter	2	egg yolks
2	Tbs. chopped onion	¾	cup freshly grated Parmesan cheese
1	cup cooked spinach, drained well and wrung in a kitchen towel	¼	pound butter, melted
½	cup ricotta cheese		Additional Parmesan cheese
½	cup flour		

1. Heat the butter in a heavy skillet. Add the onion and cook over low heat until soft. Add the cooked spinach, stirring and tossing for a few minutes until it is dry.

2. Put the spinach in a blender or food processor with the ricotta, flour, egg yolks, and Parmesan cheese. Process just until blended. Remove to a bowl and refrigerate the mixture for 1 hour.

3. Dust your hands lightly with flour and form small round dumplings about ½ inch to ¾ inch in diameter. Place the gnocchi on a large lightly floured platter. (May be prepared ahead to this point and refrigerated for several hours.

PREHEAT THE OVEN TO 400°.

4. To cook the gnocchi, bring 4 quarts of water to a boil. Gently drop in 6 or 8 gnocchi at a time. As they cook they will float to the surface; this takes 3 or 4 minutes. Remove the cooked gnocchi with a slotted spoon and place them in a large buttered baking dish. Dribble on the butter and sprinkle with additional Parmesan cheese. Bake the gnocchi in a preheated 400° oven for 5 minutes or just until the Parmesan has melted. Serve hot.

Warm Apple Fritters

SERVES 4

3	Golden Delicious apples, peeled, cored	1	egg
2	Tbs. granulated sugar	1	tsp. sugar
1	Tbs. lemon juice	½	cup all-purpose flour
2	Tbs. rum	2	cups vegetable oil
⅓	cup milk		Confectioners' sugar

1. Cut the apples horizontally into ¼-inch-thick rings. In a medium mixing bowl combine the 2 tablespoons sugar, lemon juice, and rum. Macerate the apple slices, covered, at room temperature for 1 hour.

2. Combine the milk, egg, and teaspoon of sugar in a mixing bowl. Gradually whisk in the flour until the batter is smooth. Let it rest, covered, at room temperature for 30 minutes.

3. Heat the vegetable oil in a 10-inch skillet. When it is very hot, dip the macerated apples into the batter one at a time and fry them in batches until golden on both sides. Drain on paper towels and keep warm in a 250° oven while completing recipe. Serve warm, sprinkled with confectioners' sugar.

D I N N E R 33

MELON with PROSCIUTTO

MIXED BAKED VEGETABLES GENOA STYLE

ARUGULA SALAD

ZABAGLIONE

This dinner of Italian specialties is full of robust flavors. While the mixed vegetables are baking, arrange the melon and prosciutto on chilled plates and prepare the dressing for the arugula salad. Zabaglione, which is served warm, is a last-minute effort but not a very time-consuming one.

Melon with Prosciutto · SERVES 6

1	medium cataloupe melon	6	very thin slices prosciutto
1	medium honeydew melon		Freshly ground black pepper

1. Slice the melons into thin crescents; remove the rinds and seeds.
2. Arrange alternating slices of cantaloupe and honeydew on chilled plates. Drape the prosciutto over the melon and sprinkle generously with freshly ground black pepper.

Note: If you wish to serve melon with prosciutto in the fall or winter, substitute Spanish melon for cantaloupe and honeydew.

Mixed Baked Vegetables Genoa Style   SERVES 6

This is a very satisfying main course dish based on familiar Genoese elements —potatoes, garlic, and olive oil, Also included is a heady mixture of garden-fresh vegetables baked with Parmesan cheese and herbs.

1	medium eggplant, sliced thin	2	red or green bell peppers, seeded, cut into strips
½	cup olive oil		
2	Tbs. butter	3	Tbs. fresh chopped basil leaves, or 2 tsp. dried
1	large onion, sliced thin		
2	medium potatoes, peeled, sliced thin		Salt and pepper to taste
		1	cup freshly grated Parmesan cheese
1	large clove garlic, minced		
3	small zucchini, sliced thin	½	cup fresh bread crumbs
4	firm plum tomatoes, seeded, cut into strips, or 1 ½ cups canned Italian plum tomatoes drained		

1. Sprinkle the eggplant slices with salt and let them drain, weighted (a heavy pot will do), in a colander for 40 minutes. Pat dry between paper toweling to extract as much moisture as possible. Sauté the eggplant in batches in 2 tablespoons olive oil and 2 tablespoons butter. It does not need to become crisp. Set aside.

PREHEAT THE OVEN TO 375°.

2. Oil a 2-quart baking dish or casserole with 2 tablespoons olive oil. Layer in half the vegetables, half the garlic, half the basil, 2 tablespoons olive oil, salt and pepper, and half the cheese. Repeat the layers, omitting the remaining ½ cup cheese.

3. Bake in a preheated 375° oven for 30 minutes. Sprinkle on the remaining cheese and the bread crumbs. Bake 20 minutes more. Serve hot.

Arugula Salad   SERVES 6

Arugula, sometimes called rugola, is a tender, slightly bitter salad green steadily gaining in popularity here. You'll have no trouble obtaining it from an Italian market or well-stocked greengrocer. A reasonable substitute is watercress.

3	bunches arugula	**Salt and freshly ground black**
2	Tbs. red wine vinegar	**pepper**
½	cup olive oil	

1. Trim the stems from the arugula. Rinse under running water and pat dry with paper toweling.

2. In a small bowl whisk together the vinegar and oil. Add salt and pepper to taste. Toss the arugula with the dressing just before serving.

Zabaglione   SERVES 6

This is the classic Italian wine custard. Don't let the fact that its preparation is last minute put you off. It's very easy and takes only about 10 minutes to complete.

5	egg yolks	⅓	cup dry Marsala
¼	cup sugar		

1. Put the yolks and sugar in the top part of a double boiler. Using a wire whisk or an electric beater, whip the mixture until it is pale and creamy.

2. Place over simmering water. Add the Marsala and continue beating until the mixture swells and forms soft peaks. Serve immediately in long-stemmed glasses.

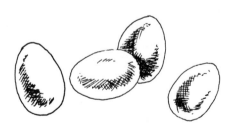

CONSOMMÉ JULIENNE

LEEK and MUSHROOM QUICHE

ASPARAGUS PUREE

STRAWBERRY RHUBARB FOOL

This menu is a delight to both the eye and the palate. Begin with a beautiful uncomplicated vegetable soup, followed by a savory leek and mushroom quiche. Pale green asparagus puree, subtle in flavor, provides just the right color contrast for the quiche. Finish off the meal with a favorite English dessert, the fruit fool.

Consommé Julienne   SERVES 4

This is a very delicate, clear vegetable soup with an almost oriental look about it. If you choose to make the soup with canned chicken broth, remove as much of the fat as possible (strain through dampened cheesecloth) and to 2½ cups broth add 2½ cups water, ½ cup chopped celery leaves, 1 parsley sprig, a pinch of thyme, and ½ bay leaf. Simmer, covered, for 20 minutes. Strain the broth and proceed as directed.

5 cups chicken stock or 2½ cups canned chicken broth combined with 2½ cups water (see above)	1 medium carrot, scraped and cut in julienne strips
	1 small leek, white part only, cut in julienne strips
½ cup canned tomatoes, drained and seeded	1 small celery stalk, cut in julienne strips
¼ tsp. dried chervil	3 mushrooms, sliced thin
¼ tsp. dried tarragon	

1. In a large saucepan simmer the chicken stock, tomatoes, and dried herbs, covered, for 30 minutes. Strain the soup and discard the tomato pulp.

2. Return the strained stock to the pan; add the julienne vegetables and sliced mushrooms. Cook, uncovered, over medium heat for 12 minutes or until the vegetables are crisp-tender. Serve hot.

Leek and Mushroom Quiche   SERVES 4–6

Both the partially baked tart shell and the filling for this quiche may be prepared in advance.

3 Tbs. butter	3 large eggs
¾ cup chopped leek, white part only	1½ cups heavy cream
	One partially baked 9-inch tart shell (p. 203)
¾ pound mushrooms, sliced thin	
2 Tbs. Madeira	¼ cup grated Swiss or Gruyère cheese
Salt and pepper to taste	

PREHEAT THE OVEN TO 400°.

1. Melt the butter in a large heavy skillet. Add the chopped leek and sauté over low heat until soft.

2. Add the mushrooms, Madeira, and salt and pepper. Cover the pan and simmer about 5 minutes.

3. Uncover the pan and cook the mixture over high heat until the liquid is reduced to 1 tablespoon. Cool slightly.

4. In a large mixing bowl whisk together the eggs and cream. Stir in the leek and mushroom mixture. (May be prepared ahead to this point and refrigerated.) Carefully pour the mixture into the prepared tart shell. Sprinkle

with grated cheese. Place the tart on a baking sheet and bake in a preheated 400° oven for 40 minutes. Serve hot or warm.

Asparagus Puree   SERVES 4

1½ pounds fresh asparagus, peeled	**2 Tbs. butter**
2 Tbs. heavy cream	**Salt and freshly ground black pepper to taste**

1. Trim the bottom of each asparagus, leaving a stalk about 5 inches long.
2. Cook the asparagus, covered, in rapidly boiling water until tender (time will depend on their size and age). Drain well and pat with paper toweling to remove excess moisture.
3. Cut the asparagus into 1-inch pieces and puree in a blender or food processor with the heavy cream.
4. Heat the butter in a saucepan, add the puree, and heat through. Season with salt and pepper. Serve hot.

Strawberry Rhubarb Fool   SERVES 4

This dessert looks so attractive, especially if it is served in a large glass bowl. The idea is to have ribbons of whipped cream running through the pureed fruit. Be sure to prepare the fool several hours ahead so that it is properly chilled when served.

1 pound rhubarb, cut into 1-inch lengths	**½ pint strawberries, hulled**
¾ cup sugar	**½ cup heavy cream, lightly whipped**

1. Combine the rhubarb and sugar in a saucepan. Cook, covered, over low heat for 20 minutes or until the rhubarb is very soft. Chill.
2. Puree the strawberries in a food processor or blender. Rub through a sieve to remove the seeds.
3. In a large bowl combine the chilled rhubarb and pureed strawberries. Fold in the whipped cream. Chill well before serving.

WATERCRESS SOUP

BROCCOLI ROULADE

BRAISED CELERY

POACHED PEARS with RASPBERRY SAUCE

When cold March winds are swirling about, your guests will be glad to sit down to a dinner like this. Begin with hot soup to warm everyone's spirits; next, serve a handsome-looking broccoli roulade along with braised celery. And end with a dessert to remind us that summer isn't *too* far away— poached pears with a very good sauce of frozen raspberries.

Watercress Soup   SERVES 6

2	Tbs. butter	5	cups heated chicken stock
1/3	cup chopped shallots or		(p. 207) or 3 cups canned
	onions		chicken broth and 2 cups
2	bunches watercress, stems		water
	trimmed	1/4	cup heavy cream
2	Tbs. flour		

1. Heat the butter in a large heavy saucepan. Add the shallots and cook over low heat until soft.

2. Add the watercress. Cook, covered, over low heat until wilted, about 5

minutes. Sprinkle on the flour and cook 3 minutes. Mixture will be gummy.

3. Gradually add the heated stock, stirring. Bring to a boil. Reduce the heat and simmer, covered, for 20 minutes. Remove the solids from the soup and puree them in a blender or food processor. Return the puree to the soup, stir in the cream, and heat through without boiling.

Broccoli Roulade   SERVES 6

A *roulade* is a soufflé baked in a large flat pan. It is then spread with a savory filling and rolled up jelly-roll fashion. You may keep the fully baked, filled roulade in a warm oven for up to an hour before serving.

FOR THE ROULADE:

Use the ingredients for the cheese soufflé (pp. 110-111).
PREHEAT THE OVEN TO 375°.

Prepare the soufflé mixture following the directions on pp. 110-111. Line a 9 × 13-inch jelly-roll pan with a well-buttered piece of foil or baking parchment. Turn the soufflé mixture into the pan, spreading it evenly. Bake in a preheated 375° oven for 20 minutes or until the soufflé is puffed and lightly browned.

FOR THE FILLING:

1	large bunch broccoli	1	clove garlic, minced
3	Tbs. butter	½	cup grated Swiss cheese
2	Tbs. chopped onion		

1. Cut the broccoli into flowerets; you should have about 4 cups. Cook the flowerets in 2 quarts of rapidly boiling water for 4 minutes. Drain well.

2. Heat the butter in a large skillet. Add the onions and cook until wilted. Add the broccoli and garlic. Cook over medium heat for 2 minutes.

3. Puree the broccoli mixture in a food processor or blender. Stir in the grated Swiss cheese.

Final assembly: Gently spread the broccoli puree evenly over the baked soufflé. Lifting the ends of the buttered foil, carefully roll the soufflé up lengthwise. If you are not planning to serve the roulade immediately, leave it on the jelly-roll pan in a warm oven; otherwise, roll it onto an attractive platter and serve with hollandaise sauce (pp. 205-206).

Braised Celery   SERVES 6

8 large ribs celery, cut into 1½-inch pieces	¼ cup canned chicken broth 1 Tbs. butter

Combine the celery and broth in a medium skillet. Simmer, covered, until the celery is crisp-tender, about 6 or 7 minutes. Stir in the butter. Serve hot.

Poached Pears with Raspberry Sauce   SERVES 6

1 cup sugar 2 quarts water Juice of 1 lemon	1 cinnamon stick 6 firm, ripe pears

1. Make the poaching syrup. Combine the sugar, water, lemon juice, and spices in a large casserole or sauté pan. Bring to a boil, lower the heat, and simmer, covered, for 20 minutes.

2. Peel the pears. Cut a slice from the bottom of each so they will stand upright. Place the pears in the poaching syrup. Cover and simmer until tender, about 40 minutes (time depends on the size and ripeness of the pears). Allow the pears to cool in the syrup before refrigerating. Chill thoroughly. Spoon raspberry sauce over each pear just before serving.

Raspberry Sauce   Makes about 1½ cups

2 10-ounce packages frozen raspberries, thawed	1 Tbs. lemon juice ½ cup black currant jelly

Drain most of the liquid from the berries and puree them in a blender or food processor. Rub the puree through a sieve to remove the seeds. Stir in the lemon juice and currant jelly. Add a little of the berry juice if the sauce seems too thick. Chill.

CONSOMMÉ à la MADRILÈNE

BAKED STUFFED ZUCCHINI

WILD RICE SALAD

THE PERFECT APPLE TART

A sparkling, cool, jellied Madrilène sets the stage for a memorable dinner, most of which is prepared in advance. Only the stuffed zucchini needs last-minute attention. And while the zucchini is baking, relax over a drink with your guests.

Consommé à la Madrilène   SERVES 4

2   cups tomato juice
½   cup chopped celery leaves
½   cup chopped onion
2   cups chicken stock (p. 207)
     or 1 cup canned chicken
     broth and 1 cup water
1   bay leaf

4   whole peppercorns
1½   Tbs. (1½ packages)
     unflavored gelatin
½   cup water
1   Tbs. dry sherry
     Watercress sprigs

1. In a saucepan combine the tomato juice, celery leaves, onion, chicken stock, bay leaf, and peppercorns. Bring to a boil. Reduce the heat and simmer, covered, for 20 minutes. Strain.

2. Sprinkle the gelatin over the water and let it soften for 10 minutes. Add the softened gelatin to the hot consommé, stirring until completely dissolved. Stir in the sherry.

3. Cool to room temperature before refrigerating. Chill the consommé until completely jelled. To serve, beat the jellied consommé lightly with a wooden spoon and serve in individual cups garnished with watercress sprigs.

Baked Stuffed Zucchini   SERVES 4

Bright green zucchini halves become a perfect container for a stuffing of mushrooms, cheese, and herbs.

4 medium zucchini, about 6 or 7 inches long	½ cup fine dry bread crumbs
Salt	¼ cup heavy cream
1 cup chopped mushrooms	1 egg, lightly beaten
3 Tbs. butter	Salt and pepper to taste
¼ cup minced shallots	Additional grated Parmesan cheese
2 Tbs. chopped parsley	
½ cup freshly grated Parmesan cheese	

1. Halve each zucchini lengthwise. Using a melon ball cutter, scoop out the flesh, leaving a thin shell. Chop the flesh, salt it lightly, and let it drain in a colander for 15 minutes. Rinse briefly and squeeze to extract excess moisture. Reserve. Blanch the zucchini shells in boiling water for 2 minutes. Drain and reserve.

2. Twist the chopped mushrooms in a kitchen towel to remove the moisture. Reserve.

3. Melt the butter in a large skillet. Add the shallots and cook until wilted. Add the zucchini flesh, mushrooms, and parsley; sauté 3 minutes. Transfer the mixture to a large bowl and stir in the remaining ingredients. Fill the reserved zucchini shells with the stuffing, mounding it slightly. (May be

prepared ahead to this point and refrigerated.)

PREHEAT THE OVEN TO 375°

4. Arrange the zucchini in a buttered baking dish, sprinkle with grated Parmesan cheese, and bake in a preheated 375° oven for 30 minutes. Serve hot with wild rice salad.

Wild Rice Salad   SERVES 4

½   cup wild rice
2   Tbs. olive oil
1¾ cups chicken stock (p. 207)
      or canned chicken broth

½   cup basic vinaigrette
      dressing (p. 206)
2   tomatoes, seeded and cubed
½   cup chopped scallions,
      including green tops

1. Rinse the rice in a colander under cold running water. Drain well.

2. Heat the olive oil in a saucepan over medium heat. Add the rice and cook, stirring, for 3 minutes or until the rice begins to darken.

3. Add the chicken stock. Bring to a boil, stirring constantly. Reduce the heat and simmer, covered, for 50 minutes or until the rice is tender. Transfer the rice to a mixing bowl.

4. While the rice is still warm, toss with ¼ cup vinaigrette dressing. Allow the rice to cool. Stir in the tomatoes and scallions. Toss with the remaining ½ cup vinaigrette. Refrigerate the salad until serving time.

The Perfect Apple Tart   SERVES 4–6

One of the all-time favorites—well browned and lightly glazed.

1   recipe pâte brisée
      sucrée (p. 203)
6   medium-sized tart apples
      (Granny Smith, Greening),
      peeled and cored

2   Tbs. sugar
1   Tbs. butter, in small pieces
      Apricot glaze (p. 206)

1. Roll the pastry dough out to a thickness of ⅛ inch. Fit it into a 9-inch tart pan with removable ring. Let rest in the refrigerator for at least 2 hours.

2. Prick the bottom of the tart shell all over with a fork. Coarsely chop 3 of the apples and spread them evenly over the tart shell. Slice the remaining apples into ¼-inch-thick slices and arrange them in a circular pattern over the chopped apples.

PREHEAT THE OVEN TO 400°.

3. Sprinkle the top of the tart with sugar; dot with butter. Bake in a preheated 400° oven for 1 hour. If the top of the tart browns too quickly, cover with foil.

4. Remove the tart from the oven and allow it to cool slightly before brushing with apricot glaze. Serve at room temperature.

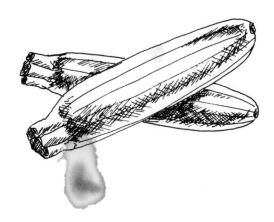

BAKED EGGPLANT

SPAGHETTI GIARDINO

ARUGULA SALAD (PP. 131-32)

FRESH FRUIT or MELON
or
TONILLE with MOCHA CREAM

This is quite a hearty meal, and my personal choice for dessert would be something simple like melon wedges with a squeeze of fresh lime. If you feel you must serve a more elaborate dessert and if calories aren't on everyone's mind, try the tonille filled with coffee-flavored whipped cream. Since you'll have to give last-minute attention to the pasta, prepare the baked eggplant ahead.

Baked Eggplant   SERVES 6

Recipes for baked eggplant abound, the most famous being Eggplant Parmigiana. One version I especially like is this one, very straightforward, made with 3 basic ingredients—eggplant, tomatoes, and Parmesan cheese.

1	eggplant, about 2 pounds, peeled and cut into ¼-inch-thick slices	2	large tomatoes, cut into ¼-inch-thick slices, seeds removed
	Salt	½	cup freshly grated Parmesan cheese
1½	cups vegetable oil	1	tsp. dried oregano
		3	Tbs. fine dry bread crumbs

PREHEAT THE OVEN TO 375°.

1. Sprinkle the sliced eggplant lightly with salt. Let drain, weighted, in a colander for 40 minutes.

2. Pat the eggplant slices dry between paper towels (really press to extract as much moisture as possible).

3. Heat the oil in a heavy 10-inch skillet. When the oil is very hot, fry 3 or 4 eggplant slices at a time, turning them until crisp and lightly browned on both sides. Remove with a slotted spoon; drain on paper towels.

4. In a lightly oiled baking dish arrange alternating layers of eggplant and tomato, adding 1 tablespoon of Parmesan cheese to each layer. (May be prepared ahead to this point.) Over the top sprinkle the oregano and bread crumbs. Bake in a preheated 375° oven for 20 minutes. May be served hot, warm, or at room temperature.

Spaghetti Giardino   SERVES 6

Pasta combines well with garden fresh vegetables. A light tomato sauce forms a liaison with crisp-tender green vegetables and lightly sautéed mushrooms. This dish must be made at the last minute because overcooking either the vegetables or the spaghetti would be ruinous. The recipe appears lengthy, but it's really not difficult. The sauce can be prepared in about 20 minutes. The pasta will cook in 6 or 7 minutes.

1	cup broccoli flowerets, cut into 1-inch-long pieces	5	medium ripe tomatoes, peeled, seeded, and cubed
2	small zucchini, cut into 2 x ¼ x ¼-inch julienne strips	1	tsp. dried basil
		1	tsp. dried oregano
6	thin asparagus, trimmed, peeled, and cut into 1-inch lengths	¼	tsp. dried red pepper flakes
		2	Tbs. minced parsley
½	cup fresh peas, shelled	1	pound thin spaghetti or vermicelli
6	Tbs. olive oil		
2	cups thinly sliced mushrooms	⅓	cup freshly grated Parmesan cheese
2	tsp. minced garlic		

1. Steam each of the green vegetables separately over boiling water until crisp-tender. Broccoli requires about 3 minutes; zucchini, 2 minutes; asparagus, 4 minutes; peas, 1 minute. Drain the vegetables well and transfer them to a large bowl.

2. Heat 2 tablespoons of the olive oil in a large heavy skillet. When the oil is quite hot, add the mushrooms and sauté 2 minutes. Add the mushrooms to the vegetable mixture.

3. In the same skillet heat the remaining 4 tablespoons of olive oil over medium heat. Add the minced garlic and chopped tomatoes. Cook, stirring, for 5 minutes. Stir in the basil, oregano, pepper flakes, and parsley. Add the reserved vegetable mixture and cook, just until heated through.

4. Cook the spaghetti in 5 quarts of rapidly boiling water until *al dente* (firm to the bite; do not overcook). Drain immediately. Transfer the spaghetti to a large bowl. Add half the vegetable sauce and toss well. Add the remaining sauce and toss again. Serve at once on warmed plates. Sprinkle each portion with freshly grated Parmesan cheese.

Tonille with Mocha Cream   SERVES 6

Crisp cookie dough disks hold a filling of flavored whipped cream.

FOR THE PASTRY:

5 ounces (10 Tbs.) butter, softened	**5 ounces toasted ground hazelnuts**
1/3 cup sugar	**1 cup all-purpose flour, sifted**

FOR THE MOCHA CREAM:

3/4 cup heavy cream	**Additional confectioners'**
2 Tbs. confectioners' sugar	**sugar**
1 Tbs. coffee extract (1 Tbs. instant coffee dissolved in 1 Tbs. cold water)	

PREHEAT THE OVEN TO 375°.

1. Prepare the pastry. With an electric beater or by hand, cream the butter and sugar until light and fluffy. Stir in the ground nuts. Add the flour and mix just until the dough begins to hold together. Do not overmix. Shape the dough into a ball, wrap in plastic, and refrigerate for at least 30 minutes.

2. Use 2 baking sheets. Cut the dough in half and place one piece on one of the baking sheets. Pat it into a round about 9 inches in diameter and 1/4 inch thick. Repeat this with the other piece of dough. Bake the pastry in a preheated 375° oven for 10 minutes or until the edges begin to brown.

3. Remove from the oven and while the pastry is still warm, trim it into a perfect circle by placing an inverted 8-inch cake tin over it. Cut each pastry disk into 6 even-sized wedges. As the pastry cools, it will become crisp. (The tonille can be prepared ahead to this point.)

The mocha cream and final assembly of the tonille should not be done more than 15 minutes before serving or the cream will become watery, and the pastry soggy. At this point, readying the dessert takes only 5 minutes.

4. Make the mocha cream. Whip the heavy cream in a well-chilled bowl using chilled beaters or a whisk. Gradually add the sugar and continue beating until the cream is stiff. Stir in the coffee extract.

5. Arrange 6 wedges of pastry on an attractive serving dish and spread the mocha cream over all. Place the remaining wedges of pastry on top so that they are lined up with the bottom wedges. Sprinkle the tonille with additional confectioners' sugar.

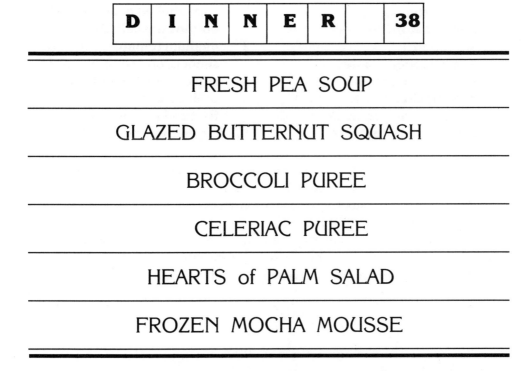

DINNER 38

FRESH PEA SOUP

GLAZED BUTTERNUT SQUASH

BROCCOLI PUREE

CELERIAC PUREE

HEARTS of PALM SALAD

FROZEN MOCHA MOUSSE

Autumn harvest colors predominate throughout this menu. For a very pretty effect serve the two pureed vegetables on the same plate as the glazed butternut squash and set out the salad in a glass bowl at the center of the table. Plan to prepare both the soup and dessert the day before.

Fresh Pea Soup   SERVES 4

A delicate-tasting puree of fresh pea soup. For added richness stir in a small amount of heavy cream.

2	Tbs. butter	3	cups shelled peas (about 3 pounds unshelled)
½	head Boston lettuce, shredded	2	medium tomatoes, peeled, seeded, and chopped, or 1 cup canned Italian tomatoes, drained and chopped
1	Tbs. chopped parsley		
½	cup chopped scallions		
4	cups chicken stock (p. 207) or 2 cups canned chicken broth and 2 cups water		Salt and pepper to taste
		¼	cup heavy cream, optional

1. Heat the butter in a large saucepan. Add the lettuce, parsley, and scallions. Sauté until the vegetables are soft.

2. Add the chicken stock, peas, and tomatoes. Simmer, covered, until the peas are tender, about 30 minutes.

3. Remove the solids from the soup and puree in a blender or food processor. Return the puree to the liquid; season with salt and pepper. If desired, stir in the cream. Heat through without boiling.

Glazed Butternut Squash   SERVES 4

1	large butternut squash, 1½ to 2 pounds	2	Tbs. brown sugar
½	tsp. allspice	2	Tbs. butter

PREHEAT THE OVEN TO 350°.

1. Peel the squash and halve it lengthwise. Remove the seeds and stringy fibers. Cut into 1½-inch cubes.

2. Turn the squash into a buttered baking dish. Sprinkle with allspice and brown sugar. Dot with 2 tablespoons of butter. Bake the squash in a preheated 350° oven for 45 minutes or until tender.

Broccoli Puree   SERVES 4

1	bunch broccoli	Salt and freshly ground black
1	Tbs. butter	pepper
2	Tbs. heavy cream	

1. Cut the broccoli into large flowerets, about 3 inches long. Trim and peel the stems and cut them into 1½-inch pieces. Cook the broccoli in boiling water to cover until tender, about 8 minutes. Drain well; reserve a tablespoon or two of the cooking liquid.

2. Puree the broccoli in a blender or food processor with a little of the cooking liquid.

3. Heat the butter in a heavy saucepan. Add the puree and stir over medium heat to evaporate most of the moisture. Stir in the heavy cream and season with salt and pepper. The puree may be kept warm over simmering water.

Celeriac Puree   SERVES 4

1½	pounds celery root		Salt and freshly ground black
1	Tbs. butter		pepper to taste
2	Tbs. heavy cream	2	Tbs. chopped parsley

1. Peel the celery root and cut it into ½-inch-thick slices. Cook in boiling water to cover until tender, about 20 minutes. Drain well. Puree in a blender or food processor.

2. Heat the butter in a heavy saucepan. Add the celeriac puree and stir over medium heat to evaporate most of the moisture. Stir in the heavy cream and season with salt and pepper. May be kept warm over simmering water. Serve garnished with chopped parsley.

Hearts of Palm Salad   SERVES 4

1   14-ounce can hearts of palm, drained and cut into ½-inch-thick slices

2   dozen cherry tomatoes, halved

2   Tbs. minced shallots
Vinaigrette dressing (p. 206)

2   Tbs. chopped parsley

Combine the hearts of palm, cherry tomatoes, and shallots in a salad bowl. Just before serving, toss with vinaigrette dressing and sprinkle on the parsley.

Frozen Mocha Mousse   SERVES 4

3   large egg yolks

3   Tbs. granulated sugar

1   Tbs. instant coffee

1   Tbs. boiling water

2   ounces semisweet chocolate (2 squares), in small pieces

¾   cup heavy cream
Confectioners' sugar to taste

1. Prepare four ¾-cup ramekins with collars to extend 2 inches above their rims.

2. Combine the egg yolks and sugar in the top of a double boiler over simmering water. Beat the mixture with a hand-held electric mixer until pale and fluffy. Remove to a bowl set over ice and beat with a whisk until the mixture is cold. Refrigerate.

3. In a small bowl dissolve the instant coffee in 1 tablespoon of boiling water. Add the chocolate pieces and stir until melted. Cool in a bowl over ice. Beat the cooled chocolate into the egg yolk mixture.

4. Beat the cream in a well-chilled bowl; add the confectioners' sugar and continue beating until stiff peaks are formed. Stir a large spoonful of cream into the chocolate mixture to lighten it. Gently fold in the remaining cream.

5. Divide the mousse evenly among the prepared ramekins and freeze for at least 2 hours or overnight. Remove the collars before serving.

TORTELLINI SALAD

ZUCCHINI with PROSCIUTTO

FONTINA-STUFFED TOMATOES

MACÉDOINE of FRESH FRUIT

In this menu attractively stuffed vegetables are preceded by a salad of tortellini garnished with fresh herbs. Dessert is sparkling fresh fruit macerated in a liqueur-flavored syrup.

Tortellini Salad   SERVES 6

Cook 1 pound of fresh or frozen tortellini in 5 quarts of rapidly boiling water until they are *al dente* (firm to the bite; do not overcook). Drain in a colander. Proceed as for ziti salad (p. 71), using the same proportions of vinegar, oil, mustard, and herbs. Omit the prosciutto. Serve the salad at room temperature.

Zucchini with Prosciutto SERVES 6

Here is another version of stuffed zucchini. This time mushrooms, onions, prosciutto, and cheese are combined to make a delicious filling for this adaptable squash.

6	medium zucchini, about 6 inches long	¾	cup chopped parsley
4	Tbs. butter	1	cup chopped prosciutto
1½	cups chopped onions	¾	cup freshly grated Parmesan cheese
1½	cups chopped mushrooms	½	cup melted butter

PREHEAT THE OVEN TO 375°.

1. Cook the zucchini in boiling water to cover for 5 minutes. Drain. Halve the zucchini lengthwise. With a melon ball cutter remove and discard the centers, leaving a ¼-inch-thick shell. Reserve.

2. Melt the butter in a large skillet over medium heat. Add the chopped onions and cook until soft. Twist the chopped mushrooms in a kitchen towel to remove the moisture. Add the mushrooms and parsley to the skillet and cook, stirring, for 4 minutes. Add the prosciutto and stir until heated through.

3. Fill the reserved zucchini halves with the mixture and arrange them in a buttered baking dish. Sprinkle each half with 1 tablespoon of grated Parmesan cheese and dribble on the butter. Bake in a preheated 375° oven for 25 minutes. Serve hot.

Fontina-stuffed Tomatoes SERVES 6

As any pizza lover knows, tomatoes and cheese have a great affinity for each other.

6	firm, ripe tomatoes	1	tsp dried oregano
	Salt		Freshly ground black pepper to taste
4	Tbs. olive oil		
½	pound diced fontina cheese		

PREHEAT THE OVEN TO 375°.

1. Slice off the top of each tomato. With a melon ball cutter scoop out and

discard the pulp and seeds. Salt the inside of the tomato shells lightly and turn them upside down on a dish. Let drain 10 minutes.

2. In a bowl combine 3 tablespoons of the olive oil with the fontina, oregano, and black pepper. Stuff the tomatoes with the mixture. Brush a baking dish with the remaining tablespoon of olive oil. Arrange the tomatoes in the dish and bake in a preheated 375° oven for 25 minutes. Serve hot.

Macédoine of Fresh Fruit   SERVES 6

½   cup sugar
½   cup fresh orange juice
¼   cup orange-flavored liqueur
     (Grand Marnier or Cointreau)

4   Valencia or navel oranges
1   pint strawberries, washed
     and hulled
2   cups cantaloupe balls

1. In a small saucepan combine the sugar and orange juice. Bring to a boil; boil 3 minutes. Away from the heat stir in the liqueur.

2. Peel and section the oranges. Remove the white pith. If the strawberries are large, halve them lengthwise; otherwise, leave whole. In a bowl combine the orange sections, strawberries, and melon balls. Pour on the liqueur-flavored syrup. Chill several hours to blend the flavors. Serve cold.

DINNER 40

CELERY SOUP

LEEKS VINAIGRETTE

MUSHROOMS MARENGO

BAKED RICE

POACHED PEARS
with RICH CHOCOLATE SAUCE

You may recognize the main course as chicken Marengo without the chicken. Mushrooms are cooked along with whole small onions in a savory white wine sauce. Serve this appealing dish piping hot with baked rice and no one will miss the chicken! The Marengo may be prepared several hours ahead and gently reheated. Soup, leeks, and dessert may all be prepared the day before.

Celery Soup SERVES 4

2	Tbs. butter		Salt and freshly ground black
2	Tbs. chopped shallots or		pepper to taste
	onions	¼	cup heavy cream
3	cups coarsely chopped celery	2	Tbs. chopped parsley
4	cups chicken stock (p. 207)		
	or 2 cups canned chicken		
	broth and 2 cups water		

1. Melt the butter in a large saucepan over medium heat. Add the shallots or onions and sauté until soft. Add the celery and cook 3 or 4 minutes.

2. Pour in the chicken stock. Bring the liquid to a boil. Reduce the heat and simmer, covered, for 40 minutes.

3. Remove the solids from the soup and puree in a blender or food processor. Return the puree to the soup, add the salt and pepper, and stir in the cream. Heat through without bringing the soup to a boil. Garnish each serving with chopped parsley.

Leeks Vinaigrette SERVES 4

Leeks are the mild-tasting members of the onion family. When cooked, their flavor becomes even milder.

8	medium-sized leeks	½	cup vinaigrette dressing (p. 206)

1. Cut away the green tops of each leek. Wash well to remove all traces of sand.

2. In a saucepan bring enough water to a boil to cover the leeks when added. Add the leeks, reduce the heat, and simmer, covered, for 18 to 20 minutes. Drain well and cool.

3. Arrange the leeks in a shallow dish; pour on the vinaigrette. Marinate 1 hour at room temperature, then refrigerate. Serve cold.

Mushrooms Marengo   SERVES 4

6	Tbs. butter	1½	cups canned tomatoes, drained and chopped
¾	pound small white onions, peeled	1	Tbs. tomato paste
1½	pounds small mushrooms, trimmed	1	bay leaf
		½	tsp. thyme
½	cup chopped onions	1	clove garlic, crushed
2	Tbs. flour		Freshly ground black pepper to taste
1	cup chicken stock (p. 207) or canned chicken broth		
¾	cup white wine	2	Tbs. chopped parsley

1. Melt 3 tablespoons of the butter in a large skillet over medium heat. Add the white onions and brown lightly. Remove to a bowl with a slotted spoon. Add the mushrooms to the skillet; sauté until browned. Remove to a bowl.

2. Heat the remaining 3 tablespoons of butter in a 4-quart casserole. Add the chopped onions; sauté until wilted. Sprinkle on the flour and stir over low heat for 3 minutes. Slowly add the chicken stock and wine. Stir the mixture until smooth and slightly thickened. Add the tomatoes, tomato paste, bay leaf, thyme, garlic, and black pepper.

3. Add the reserved white onions and mushrooms to the casserole. Cover and simmer 25 minutes or until the onions are tender. Stir in the chopped parsley. Serve hot.

Baked Rice   SERVES 4

2½	Tbs. butter	1	cup chicken broth
2	Tbs. minced shallots or onions	½	cup water
		¼	tsp. dried basil
1	cup rice	1	small bay leaf

PREHEAT THE OVEN TO 400°.

1. Heat the butter in a heavy saucepan. Add the shallots or onions and cook until wilted. Add the rice and stir until it is well coated with butter.

2. Stir in the chicken broth, water, and herbs. Bring the liquid to a boil. Cover the pan and place in a preheated 400° oven. Bake 18 minutes. Remove and fluff with a fork. If not served immediately, the rice may be kept warm, covered, for about 15 minutes.

Poached Pears with Rich Chocolate Sauce   SERVES 4

I think you'll enjoy the contrast of cold poached pears served with warm chocolate sauce.

4   pears poached according to   **Rich chocolate sauce**
directions on p. 138   **(pp. 81-82)**

Arrange the pears on each of 4 plates and dribble over them a spoonful or two of warm chocolate sauce.

APPLE CRÊPES with ROQUEFORT SAUCE

WILD RICE SALAD (P. 141)
or
SPINACH-MUSHROOM SALAD (PP. 60-61)

PLATTER of ASSORTED CHEESES

This is a light meal that could be planned for late supper or Sunday brunch. If the crêpes are prepared ahead and the apples peeled and sliced, there will be little last-minute work. (To prevent discoloration, sprinkle the sliced apples with lemon juice and refrigerate, covered.) You can have the Roquefort sauce ready in less time than it takes for the crêpes to heat through. Either of the salads mentioned above will complement the meal nicely.

At the end of this menu I've listed the names of several cheeses. Choose the ones that appeal to you most and serve them on an attractive platter. Offer sliced French bread or plain crisp biscuits.

Apple Crêpes with Roquefort Sauce   SERVES 4

| 3 | Tbs. butter | 8 | crêpes (p. 203) |
| 5 | Golden Delicious apples, peeled, cored, and cut into ¼-inch-thick slices | | |

FOR THE ROQUEFORT SAUCE:

¼	pound Roquefort cheese	2	Tbs. butter
⅓	cup milk	¼	cup heavy cream

PREHEAT THE OVEN TO 400°.

1. Heat the butter in a large heavy skillet. Sauté the sliced apples until lightly browned. Remove to a dish.

2. Place equal portions of sautéed apples in the center of each crêpe; fold and roll to enclose the filling. Arrange the crêpes in a buttered baking dish. Bake 15 minutes in a preheated 400° oven. Serve with Roquefort sauce.

3. In a small heavy saucepan combine the Roquefort, milk, and butter. Cook over low heat, stirring, just until the cheese melts and the sauce is smooth. Stir in the heavy cream and heat through, stirring constantly. The sauce may be kept warm over very low heat.

Platter of Assorted Cheeses

To appreciate its full flavor and aroma, you should serve cheese at room temperature. Remove from the refrigerator at least 45 minutes before serving. Here are some suggestions.

The "Swiss" cheeses: Appenzeller, Emmentaler, Gruyère, Jarlsberg.

French soft-ripened cheeses: Brie, Camembert.

French cream cheeses: Brillat-Savarin, L'Explorateur, St. André. Unbelievably smooth and spreadable. The ultimate cream cheeses.

Mild semisoft Dutch cheeses: Edam, Gouda.

Cheddars from Canada, England, New York, and Vermont. Ranging in flavor from very sharp to very mild. May be quite smooth or hard and crumbly.

Cheshire, a cheddarlike, crumbly cheese from England.

Italian fontina, mildly flavored; has the texture of Edam and Gouda.

MARINATED MUSHROOMS

ONION-PEPPER FRITTATA

GREEN SALAD

ALMOND MERINGUES

Another good late supper menu, with only the salad requiring last-minute tossing. Fresh fruit in season would be an appropriate way to end this meal, but I have included a recipe for almond meringues in case someone has a very sweet tooth. Serve the fruit too!

Marinated Mushrooms   SERVES 6

1¼ pound small white
     mushrooms, stems trimmed
1½ cups water
1½ cups white vinegar
4   whole cloves, 6 whole
     peppercorns, ¼ tsp. mustard
     seed, ¼ tsp. dried rosemary,
     and 1 bay leaf tied in a
     cheesecloth bag

½ cup olive oil
½ tsp. oregano
1 clove garlic crushed
   Salt and freshly ground black
   pepper to taste

1. Put the mushrooms in a saucepan (nonaluminum) with the water, vinegar, and the herbs tied in cheesecloth. Bring to a boil. Cover the pan and cook at a slow boil for 5 or 6 minutes.

2. Transfer the mushrooms and their cooking liquid to a bowl. Marinate, covered, at room temperature 2 hours.

3. Drain the mushrooms and pat dry with paper toweling. Place in a bowl and pour on the olive oil. Add the oregano, garlic, and salt and pepper. Toss to coat. Let the mushrooms steep in olive oil for a few hours before serving. Good either cold or at room temperature.

Onion-Pepper Frittata   SERVES 6

An Italian frittata tastes like an omelette and looks like a crustless quiche. Unlike an omelette, however, a frittata takes about 30 minutes to prepare, but like a quiche, it can be made ahead of time (but not reheated) and served at room temperature.

¼	cup olive oil	6	Tbs. freshly grated Parmesan
1	cup thinly sliced onions		cheese
2	medium red or green bell peppers, seeded and sliced thin	½	tsp. dried basil
		1	Tbs. chopped parsley
		4	Tbs. butter
6	large eggs		

1. Heat the oil in a medium-sized skillet. Add the onions and peppers and sauté until wilted.

2. Beat the eggs lightly with a whisk. Add the onion-pepper mixture and 4 tablespoons of the Parmesan cheese. Stir in the basil and parsley.

3. Heat the butter in a 10-inch black iron skillet. When it begins to foam, pour in the egg mixture. Cook over very low heat for 20 minutes or just until the eggs have set.

4. Over the top sprinkle the remaining 2 tablespoons of Parmesan cheese. Run the frittata under a preheated broiler for 30 to 45 seconds to set the top. Loosen the edge of the frittata with a spatula and slide it onto a platter. Serve hot or at room temperature with a green salad tossed with vinaigrette dressing (p. 206).

Almond Meringues

This recipe makes approximately 24 to 26 meringues, each about 3 inches wide. Leftover meringues will stay crisp for up to a month if sealed well and stored in a dry place.

4	ounces ground blanched almonds (almond flour)	1½	Tbs. cornstarch
⅓	cup granulated sugar	4	egg whites
		½	cup granulated sugar

PREHEAT THE OVEN TO 275°.

1. In a mixing bowl combine the almond flour, ⅓ cup sugar, and the cornstarch. Mix with your hands to blend well. Set aside.

2. Beat the egg whites in the bowl of an electric mixer until stiff peaks are formed. Add ½ cup sugar and continue beating 10 seconds longer.

3. Fold the almond flour mixture rapidly into the egg whites. Line 2 baking sheets with parchment paper. Fill a pastry bag fitted with a no. 4 plain tube with the meringue and pipe out round or oval shapes about 3 inches wide. Bake in a preheated 275° oven for 60 to 70 minutes. The meringues will be a *very* pale brown color. Let cool until crisp, then carefully remove from the parchment.

RED PEPPER SOUP

BROCCOLI TIMBALES with TOMATO SAUCE

SWEET-and-SOUR ONIONS

BAKED APPLES

An ambitious menu for a special occasion. Delicate, jewellike timbales of broccoli are served with a simple tomato sauce and accompanied by piquant sweet-and-sour onions. The first course is a beautiful orange-red pepper soup (prepared ahead); dessert, a time-honored favorite—baked apples.

To avoid a lot of last-minute work, plan to prepare the apples and tomato sauce the day before. The timbale mixture (cream, eggs, and broccoli) may be prepared hours in advance of cooking. The onions, too, may be readied ahead and gently reheated.

Red Pepper Soup   SERVES 4

The color of this soup is really quite arresting. Use the reddest bell peppers you can find.

2	Tbs. butter	4	cups heated chicken stock (p. 207) or 2 cups canned chicken broth and 2 cups water
½	cup chopped onion		
1	pound red bell peppers, peeled, seeded, and cut into 1-inch strips	1	Tbs. tomato paste
1	Tbs. flour	1	tsp. paprika
		1	Tbs. dry vermouth
		¼	cup heavy cream

1. Melt the butter in a heavy saucepan over low heat. Add the onion and cook until wilted. Add the peppers and cook until soft, about 8 minutes.

2. Sprinkle on the flour and stir over medium heat for 3 minutes. Slowly pour in the heated stock. Stir to blend. Add the tomato paste and paprika. Bring the liquid to a boil. Reduce the heat and simmer, covered, for 30 minutes.

3. Remove the solids from the soup and puree in a blender or food processor. Return the puree to the liquid, stir in the vermouth and heavy cream. Heat through without bringing the soup to a boil.

Broccoli Timbales with Tomato Sauce   SERVES 4

2	cups broccoli flowerets	4	eggs
1	Tbs. butter		Salt and freshly ground black pepper to taste
2	Tbs. chopped onion		
1	cup heavy cream	¼	cup grated Swiss cheese

PREHEAT THE OVEN TO 375°.

1. Blanch the broccoli flowerets in boiling water for 1 minute. Drain and pat dry. Chop the broccoli fine.

2. Heat the butter in a skillet. Add the onion and sauté until wilted. Stir in the chopped broccoli and heat through for a minute.

3. In a bowl whisk together the cream and eggs, salt and pepper. Add the Swiss cheese and broccoli. (May be prepared ahead to this point.)

4. Butter the insides of four ¾-cup ramekins. Line the bottoms with rounds of buttered baking parchment. Pour in the broccoli mixture. Place the ramekins in a pan and add enough water to come halfway up the sides. Bake

in a preheated 375° oven for 20 to 25 minutes or until the mixture pulls away from the sides of the molds. Unmold, remove the parchment, and serve with fresh tomato sauce (recipe follows).

Fresh Tomato Sauce   Makes about 1½ cups

1	Tbs. butter	4	medium tomatoes, peeled, seeded, and chopped (about 2 cups)
2	Tbs. minced shallots		Salt and freshly ground black pepper to taste

1. Heat the butter in a small heavy saucepan. Add the shallots and cook until soft.

2. Add the tomatoes and salt and pepper. Cook, uncovered, over low heat for 30 minutes. Puree the mixture in a blender or food processor. Heat through gently before serving. This is good over pasta too.

Sweet-and-Sour Onions   SERVES 4

1	pound small white onions, peeled	1	tsp. sugar
3	Tbs. butter, in small pieces		Salt and freshly ground black pepper to taste
2	Tbs. white wine vinegar		

1. Put the onions and butter in a large heavy skillet. Add enough water to come half an inch up the side of the pan. Cook over medium heat for 20 minutes. Stir occasionally.

2. Add the vinegar, sugar, and salt and pepper. Cook, covered, over low heat until the onions are well browned and tender, about 45 minutes. Stir from time to time to prevent sticking and add a tablespoon or two of water if the cooking liquid is reducing too rapidly. Serve hot.

Baked Apples   SERVES 4

An all-American classic.

4 **large tart apples**	**4** **Tbs. butter**
¼ **cup brown sugar mixed with**	**1** **cup apple cider or apple juice**
½ tsp. ground cinnamon	

PREHEAT THE OVEN TO 375°.

1. Core the apples, taking care not to cut all the way through to the bottom.

2. Arrange the apples in a buttered baking dish and fill each of the cavities with the sugar-cinnamon mixture and 1 tablespoon of butter. Pour in the cider or juice. Bake in a preheated 375° oven for 45 minutes or until the apples are soft but still retain their shape. Serve at room temperature or lightly chilled.

BAKED OYSTERS

SPAGHETTI with ZUCCHINI SAUCE

GREEN SALAD with GORGONZOLA SAUCE

PEACHES au GRATIN

I think it's great fun to begin an otherwise simple menu with an extravagant first course. Actually, you don't have to feel too guilty about the cost of the oysters because the rest of the meal is in the budget category.

The oysters should be served as soon as they emerge from the oven, but the flavored crumbs under which they're baked can be made ahead of time; likewise, the dessert and salad dressing. At serving time make the quickly prepared zucchini sauce and cook the spaghetti.

Baked Oysters   SERVES 4

Plump fresh oysters baked briefly under a sprinkling of flavored crumbs and cheese. Take care not to overcook the oysters.

6	Tbs. butter	2	Tbs. chopped parsley
2	cloves garlic, minced	20	fresh shucked oysters
1½	cups fresh bread crumbs (made from a good Italian bread)	3	Tbs. freshly grated Parmesan cheese

PREHEAT THE OVEN TO **450°**.

1. Heat 4 tablespoons of the butter in a heavy skillet over medium heat. Briefly sauté the garlic; it must not brown. Add the bread crumbs and fry, stirring constantly, for about 2 minutes or until the crumbs are golden brown. Stir in the parsley. Set aside.

2. Butter a baking dish that will later accommodate the oysters in a single layer. Spread one-third of the crumbs in the dish; arrange the oysters on top. Add the Parmesan cheese to the remaining crumbs and sprinkle this over the oysters. Dot with the remaining 2 tablespoons of butter and bake in a pre-heated 450° oven for 8 minutes—not longer or the oysters will toughen. Serve immediately.

Spaghetti with Zucchini Sauce SERVES 4

2	Tbs. butter	1	large clove garlic, minced
2	Tbs. olive oil	2	Tbs. chopped parsley
2	anchovy fillets, chopped	1	pound spaghetti
4	small zucchini, cut into 2 x ¼ x ¼-inch julienne strips	¼	cup freshly grated Parmesan cheese
2	medium tomatoes, peeled, seeded, and chopped		

1. Heat the butter and oil in a large heavy skillet. Add the chopped anchovies and stir once. Add the zucchini and cook, stirring occasionally, for 2 minutes.

2. Add the tomatoes. Add the garlic. Cook the mixture over low heat until the tomatoes are soft. Stir in the parsley. Keep the sauce warm over very low heat.

3. Cook the spaghetti in 5 quarts of rapidly boiling water until *al dente* (firm to the bite; do not overcook). Drain well in a colander. Transfer the spaghetti to a large heated bowl. Toss with the zucchini sauce. Add the Parmesan cheese and toss again. Serve immediately on warmed plates.

Green Salad with Gorgonzola Dressing   SERVES 4

1   small head romaine lettuce,   ½   cup light olive oil
    rinsed and dried well   Freshly ground black pepper
1   small red onion, sliced thin   to taste
2   Tbs. red wine vinegar   ¼   pound Gorgonzola cheese,
                                           softened

1. Tear the lettuce into bite-sized pieces. Combine with the sliced onions in a salad bowl.

2. Whisk together the vinegar, oil, and pepper. Stir in the cheese with a fork, breaking up the lumps. Toss the salad with dressing just before serving.

Peaches au Gratin   SERVES 4

½   cup crushed amaretti (Italian   3   Tbs. butter, softened
    macaroons)   4   firm, ripe peaches, halved
¼   tsp. ground cinnamon   and pitted
1   Tbs. sugar

PREHEAT THE OVEN TO 375°.

1. In a small bowl work the amaretti, cinnamon, sugar, and butter with your fingertips until well combined. Spoon equal portions of the mixture over each peach half, forcing it into the hollows.

2. Arrange the peaches in a buttered baking dish. Bake in a preheated 375° oven for 30 minutes or until the tops of the peaches are lightly browned. Cool on a wire rack. Serve the peaches at room temperature.

ENDIVE-WATERCRESS SALAD (P. 89)

STUFFED CABBAGE ROLLS

SWEET-and-SOUR ONIONS (P. 165)
or
DILLED BEETS

APPLE CLAFOUTI

This menu brings together a diverse selection of dishes comprised of winter vegetables. Open the meal with a crisp salad of endive and watercress. Next come hearty cabbage rolls stuffed with rice, mixed vegetables, and a touch of cheese. Choose either sweet-and-sour onions or dilled beets to accompany the cabbage. The meal ends on a sweet note with an easily made apple dessert that goes into the oven along with the cabbage rolls.

Stuffed Cabbage Rolls   SERVES 4

8	large cabbage leaves	½	cup grated Swiss cheese
3	Tbs. butter	½	tsp. dried thyme
½	cup chopped onion		Salt and freshly ground black
½	cup chopped celery		pepper to taste
1½	cups sliced mushrooms	1	16-ounce can plum tomatoes
1	cup cooked rice	1	bay leaf

PREHEAT THE OVEN TO 350°.

1. Plunge the cabbage leaves into boiling water to cover for 3 minutes. Remove and drain. Dry well between paper towels. Cut away the woody stems at the base of each leaf.

2. Heat the butter in a skillet. Sauté the onion and celery until wilted. Remove to a bowl with a slotted spoon.

3. If necessary, add more butter to the skillet and cook the mushrooms over high heat, stirring and tossing for 2 minutes. Add the mushrooms to the onion and celery. Add the rice, Swiss cheese, thyme, and salt and pepper. Combine the mixture well.

4. Divide the rice mixture evenly among the cabbage leaves; roll to enclose the filling. (May be prepared ahead to this point.) Lightly butter an oven-proof baking dish; in it arrange the cabbage rolls seam side down in a single layer. Halve the tomatoes and add them with their juice to the baking dish. Put in the bay leaf. Bake in a preheated 350° oven for 50 minutes. Serve hot.

Dilled Beets   SERVES 4

1	pound fresh beets	Salt and freshly ground black
2	Tbs. butter, softened	pepper to taste
2	Tbs. minced fresh dill	

1. Cut away the beet tops, leaving about 1 inch of stem above the bulb. Do not peel.

2. Cook the beets in boiling water to cover for 35 to 45 minutes or until tender. The cooking time depends on their size. Drain and cool slightly. Peel the beets and slice thin. Remove to a warmed vegetable dish and toss with butter, dill, and salt and pepper.

Apple Clafouti   SERVES 4 – 6

3	Tbs. butter	¼	tsp. ground cinnamon
1	pound tart apples, peeled, cored, and cut into ¼-inch-thick slices	1	cup milk
		½	cup granulated sugar
2	Tbs. dark rum	3	eggs
	Grated zest of ½ lemon	⅔	cup all-purpose flour, sifted
			Confectioners' sugar

PREHEAT THE OVEN TO 350°.

1. Heat the butter in a large skillet, add the apples, and sauté over medium heat until lightly browned. Remove to a bowl; season with rum, lemon zest, and cinnamon.

2. Place the remaining ingredients (except the confectioners' sugar) in a blender or food processor. Process the batter until smooth.

3. Butter the bottom and sides of a deep 8-inch pie pan. Spread the apples over the bottom of the pan; pour the batter over all. Bake the clafouti in a preheated 350° oven for 1 hour or until a knife inserted down the middle comes out clean. Serve warm dusted with confectioners' sugar.

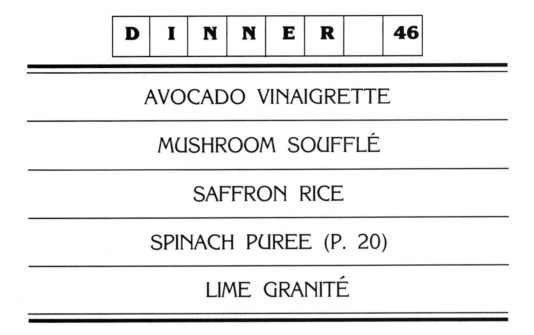

AVOCADO VINAIGRETTE

MUSHROOM SOUFFLÉ

SAFFRON RICE

SPINACH PUREE (P. 20)

LIME GRANITÉ

Everyone's immediate reaction to this menu is one of great pleasure—and no wonder. The airy mushroom soufflé looks splendid flanked by pale yellow rice and bright green spinach. The meal begins with an easy first course (no cooking) and ends with refreshing lime granité, which has been prepared ahead.

Avocado Vinaigrette   SERVES 4

2   medium-sized ripe   Vinaigrette dressing (p. 206)
    avocados

Halve the avocados and remove their pits. Just before serving spoon a tablespoon or two of vinaigrette dressing into the hollow of each half.

Mushroom Soufflé   SERVES 4

¾	pound fresh mushrooms, chopped	⅛	tsp. black pepper
1	cup milk	⅛	tsp. ground nutmeg
2	Tbs. butter	5	egg whites, at room temperature, stiffly beaten
3	Tbs. flour		Bread crumbs
4	egg yolks, at room temperature	2	Tbs. freshly grated Parmesan cheese
1	Tbs. Madeira		

PREHEAT THE OVEN TO 375°.

1. Put the mushrooms and milk in a saucepan. Bring to a boil. Lower the heat and simmer 12 minutes.

2. In a heavy saucepan melt the butter. Add the flour and stir the *roux* over low heat for 2 minutes. Stir in the mushrooms and milk. Cook the sauce, stirring constantly, for 5 minutes. The sauce will be very thick. Away from the heat, beat in the yolks, one at a time. Stir in the Madeira, black pepper, and nutmeg. (May be prepared ahead to this point.)

3. Fold about one-quarter of the egg whites into the sauce to lighten it. Gently fold in the remaining egg whites.

4. Butter the bottom and sides of a 1½-quart soufflé case; sprinkle with fine dry bread crumbs. Pour in the soufflé mixture; sprinkle the top with Parmesan cheese. Bake the soufflé in a preheated 375° oven for 30 minutes or until puffed and golden. Serve immediately.

Saffron Rice   SERVES 4

1	Tbs. butter	1	cup rice
2	Tbs. chopped onion	1	cup water
¼	tsp. saffron	½	cup canned chicken broth

1. Heat the butter in a 2-quart saucepan. Add the onion and sauté until soft. Stir in the saffron.

2. Add the rice; stir a few moments until the rice is coated with butter. Add the water and chicken broth. Bring to a boil. Cover, reduce the heat, and simmer 18 minutes.

Lime Granité   SERVES 4

4 large limes	**½ cup fresh lime juice**
1½ cups water	**Grated zest of 1 large lime**
¾ cup sugar	**Fresh mint**

1. Cut a slice off the top of each lime. Remove the pulp and reserve ½ cup lime juice and the hollowed-out lime shells.

2. In a saucepan bring the water and sugar to a boil. Boil the syrup for 5 minutes. Let cool. Stir in the reserved ½ cup lime juice and the lime zest. Pour the mixture into a metal ice cube tray (without the dividers) and freeze until mushy.

3. Transfer the ice to a chilled bowl and beat it thoroughly with an electric mixer. Return the mixture to the ice cube tray and freeze until firm or overnight. To serve, fill the reserved lime shells with equal portions of ice, and if desired, garnish with fresh mint.

| D | I | N | N | E | R | | 47 |

HOT BORSCHT (PP. 33-34)

BLINI with CAVIAR and SMOKED SALMON

APRICOTS in COGNAC (PP. 35-36)
or
ALMOND MERINGUES (P. 162)

Invite two close friends to share the ultimate late night supper—yeasty blini served with caviar and smoked salmon. Drink champagne! If the pocketbook can take it, serve apricots in cognac for dessert; otherwise, almond meringues will do nicely. Offer espresso in demitasses with dessert.

Blini with Caviar and Smoked Salmon   SERVES 4

1¼	cups lukewarm milk	1	extra-large egg, lightly
1½	tsp. dry yeast		beaten
½	cup all-purpose flour, sifted		Sour cream
½	cup buckwheat flour, sifted	½	pound smoked salmon
1½	Tbs. granulated sugar	¼	pound salmon caviar
¼	tsp. salt		Additional melted butter
3	Tbs. melted butter		

1. In a small bowl combine the warm milk and yeast. Stir until the yeast dissolves.

2. In a large bowl mix together the two flours, sugar, and salt. Stir in the dissolved yeast, melted butter, and egg. Whisk the mixture until it is free of lumps. Cover with a damp cloth and let stand in a warm place for 1½ hours.

3. Lightly butter a small heavy skillet or crêpe pan. Set it over medium heat. Pour about 3 tablespoons of batter into the pan and fry the blini until golden brown on each side. Keep warm in a 300° oven until all the batter has been used.

Yield: 12 to 15 blini.

To serve: Place a dollop of sour cream on each blini, add either caviar or smoked salmon, roll to enclose the filling, and pour on a little melted butter.

CITRUS FRUIT CUP

CROQUE MADAME

GREEN SALAD (optional)

APPLE QUICHE

FRESHLY BREWED COFFEE and TEA

Brunch with friends. Relaxed, cozy, informal. Have a large pot of freshly brewed coffee ready. And also offer freshly brewed tea (perhaps smoky lapsang souchong). Start taste buds tingling with zesty citrus fruit cup and follow that with *croque madame*—hot open-faced cheese sandwiches. A fresh green salad is always welcome, but not absolutely necessary; the choice is up to you. End the meal with an apple custard dessert baked in a buttery pastry shell. Fruit cup and apple quiche may both be prepared ahead of time.

Citrus Fruit Cup   SERVES 6

2   medium grapefruit
4   large oranges (navel or Temple)
4   tangerines, peeled and sectioned

½   cup freshly squeezed orange juice
     Fresh mint sprigs

1. Cut the grapefruit and oranges in half. Section and separate the fruit from the white membranes with a grapefruit knife. Remove any pits. Transfer the fruit to a bowl.

2. Add the tangerine sections to the bowl. Pour on the orange juice. Serve well chilled, garnished with mint sprigs.

Croque Madame   SERVES 6

Here is the French version of the grilled cheese sandwich.

¼	cup milk	1	Tbs. cognac
2	Tbs. flour		Pinch of cayenne pepper
½	tsp. baking powder	6	thick slices of day-old challa
½	pound sharp cheddar cheese		bread (braided egg bread) or
	or Swiss cheese, grated		*pain brioche*
4	eggs		

PREHEAT THE BROILER.

1. In a mixing bowl whisk together the milk, flour, and baking powder. Whisk in the cheese, eggs, cognac, and cayenne. Blend thoroughly. The batter should be smooth. If preferred, blend the above ingredients in a blender or food processor. (May be prepared up to 2 hours ahead to this point; cover but do not refrigerate.)

2. Arrange the bread on a buttered baking sheet. Spread equal portions of cheese batter over each slice. Place the baking sheet under the broiler about 5 inches from the heat source. Toast the sandwiches for 3 or 4 minutes (watch closely to avoid burning) or until nicely browned on top. Let cool. Cut each *croque* in half diagonally.

Apple Quiche   SERVES 6

3	large eggs	2	large apples, about 1 pound
½	cup sugar		(Golden Delicious or Granny
1½	cups heavy cream		Smith), peeled, cored, and
¼	tsp. vanilla		diced
		1	partially baked 9-inch sweet
			pastry shell (p. 203)
			Confectioners' sugar

PREHEAT THE OVEN TO 400°.

1. Beat the eggs and sugar together in a large bowl using a wire whisk. Slowly whisk in the cream. Stir in the vanilla.

2. Spread the diced apples evenly over the bottom of the partially baked tart shell. Pour in the cream mixture.

3. Bake the quiche in a preheated 400° oven for 25 to 30 minutes or until the custard is set. Remove from the oven and cool on a wire rack. Dust with confectioners' sugar. Serve warm or at room temperature.

OLD-FASHIONED POTATO PANCAKES

HOMEMADE APPLESAUCE

FAVORITE CHOCOLATE BROWNIES

Here's a quick supper menu—the sort of meal kids love to eat—but grown-ups don't have to be excluded. Gather around the kitchen table and eat the pancakes hot out of the pan. Serve with homemade applesauce and sour cream. If you would like a salad, marinated cucumbers (p. 69) would be a good choice. Brownies need no introduction other than to say "they're irresistible."

Old-fashioned Potato Pancakes   SERVES 4

2½	cups peeled, grated potatoes (baking potatoes are good for this)	2	Tbs. matzoh meal or fine cracker crumbs
2	large eggs	3	Tbs. grated onion
			Salt to taste
		¾	cup vegetable oil

1. Wring the grated potatoes in a kitchen towel to extract as much moisture as possible. Remove to a bowl. Stir in the eggs, matzoh meal, and onion. Add salt if desired.

2. Heat the oil in a heavy skillet over medium-high heat. Drop the pan-

181

cake mixture by spoonfuls into hot oil, forming pancakes about 3 inches in diameter. Fry on both sides until golden brown. Serve hot with applesauce and sour cream.

Homemade Applesauce   Makes about 3 cups

This, of course, is great for dessert, served warm with a little heavy cream. Or serve it cold with the Thanksgiving turkey.

6 large apples (I like a combination of tart and sweet), peeled, cored, and cubed	**3 Tbs. water**
	2 Tbs. butter
	½ tsp. ground cinnamon

1. Put the apples and water in a large saucepan. Cover and simmer for 25 minutes or until the apples are very soft.
2. Transfer the apples to a mixing bowl. Add the butter and cinnamon. Beat with a wooden spoon until the mixture is smooth. Serve warm or chilled.

Favorite Chocolate Brownies

This recipe makes about 30 brownies. Wrap leftovers individually in plastic wrap; they'll stay fresh and moist several days. May also be frozen.

4 ounces (4 squares) unsweetened chocolate	**½ tsp. vanilla**
6 Tbs. butter	**½ cup all-purpose flour, sifted**
2 eggs, at room temperature	**½ cup chopped walnuts (optional)**
1 cup granulated sugar	

PREHEAT THE OVEN TO 350°.
1. Melt the chocolate and butter together in a large heavy saucepan over very low heat. Let cool slightly.

2. Beat in the eggs, sugar, and vanilla. Fold in the flour, blending thoroughly. Stir in the nuts if you are using them.

3. Butter the bottom and sides of a 9-inch square baking pan. Line the bottom of the pan with parchment; butter the parchment. Turn the batter into the pan. Bake in a preheated 350° oven for 25 minutes. Cool. Remove from the pan, lift away the parchment, and cut the cake into squares.

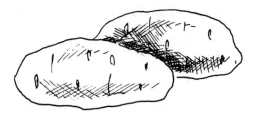

PUNGENT EGGPLANT from KASHMIR

CAULIFLOWER CURRY

CUCUMBER RAITA

SAFFRON RICE (P. 174)

FRESH SLICED MANGO
or
LIME GRANITÉ (P. 175)

This menu of fragrantly spiced dishes has an Indian accent. To start, a marvelous eggplant appetizer (can be made ahead) with a pungent, spicy flavor—a little difficult to describe—you must try it. The main course is a cauliflower curry (not too spicy) served with pilaf and yogurt sauce. The lime granité brings the meal to a refreshing close. The yogurt sauce and dessert may both be prepared ahead; simmer the pilaf while the curry is in the oven.

Pungent Eggplant from Kashmir   SERVES 4

An exotic combination of eggplant, spices, and fresh ginger.

½	cup vegetable oil	1	tsp. paprika
1	eggplant (about 1 pound), cut into thin strips	¼	tsp. hot red pepper flakes
		¼	cup fresh chopped ginger
1	whole clove	1	cup ripe tomatoes, peeled, seeded, and cubed
1	cup chopped onion		
1	clove garlic, chopped	½	cup water

1. Heat the oil in a large heavy saucepan. Fry the eggplant in batches until the flesh is browned and the skin wrinkled. Remove to a bowl with a slotted spoon.

2. To the saucepan add the clove, chopped onion, and garlic. Sauté until lightly browned. Stir in the paprika, red pepper flakes, and ginger. Cook, stirring often, over low heat about 8 minutes. Add the tomatoes and cook until they are soft; stir occasionally to prevent sticking (it may be necessary to add a tablespoon or two of water).

3. Return the eggplant to the saucepan and add ½ cup water. Cover and simmer until the eggplant is very tender, about 20 minutes. May be served hot, warm, or at room temperature.

Cauliflower Curry   SERVES 4

1	cup vegetable oil	½	cup canned tomatoes and ½ cup of their liquid
1	large cauliflower (about 1½ to 2 pounds), cut into flowerets		
		½	tsp. ground cumin
		½	tsp. ground cardamom
1½	cups chopped onion	½	tsp. ground turmeric
¼	cup fresh coriander, chopped	1	clove garlic, crushed
¼	tsp. hot red pepper flakes	1	bay leaf
		1	cup fresh peas

PREHEAT THE OVEN TO 350°.

1. Heat the oil in a large casserole over medium heat. Sauté the cauliflower flowerets until lightly browned. Remove to a bowl with a slotted spoon.

2. In a blender or food processor puree the onion, coriander, red pepper flakes, and tomatoes with their juice. Cook the puree in the casserole over medium heat until it is thickened, about 10 minutes. Stir in the remaining

spices and garlic and return the cauliflower to the casserole. Stir in the peas. Cover and bake in a preheated 350° oven for 20 minutes. Serve hot with cucumber raita.

Cucumber Raita   Makes about 1½ cups

This is a traditional Indian yogurt sauce that is both cool and spicy at the same time.

1	large cucumber, peeled, seeded, and coarsely grated	1	tsp. fresh minced hot chili pepper
¼	tsp. ground cumin	1	cup yogurt
		1	Tbs. fresh minced coriander

In a bowl combine the cucumber, cumin, and hot chili pepper. Stir in the yogurt and fresh coriander. Refrigerate until serving time.

| D | I | N | N | E | R | | 51 |

BEAN SPROUT and WATERCRESS SALAD

STIR-FRIED VEGETABLES

RICE with TOMATO FLAVOR

CHOCOLATE ORANGES

This is a quick light meal that you can have on the table in under an hour's time (that does not include dessert, which should be made ahead).

Bean Sprout and Watercress Salad   SERVES 6

A delightfully crunchy salad in a soy vinaigrette dressing.

1¼	pounds bean sprouts, rinsed and dried well	3	Tbs. soy sauce
1	bunch watercress, rinsed, trimmed, and dried well	2	Tbs. peanut oil
		1	Tbs. oriental sesame oil
2	Tbs. rice wine vinegar	1	clove garlic, crushed

1. Combine the bean sprouts and watercress in a salad bowl.

2. In a small bowl whisk together the vinegar, soy sauce, peanut and sesame oils. Stir in the garlic. Pour the dressing over the salad just before serving.

Stir-fried Vegetables SERVES 6

1/3 Tbs. oriental sesame oil	1 large clove garlic, minced
2 large ribs celery, cut diagonally into 1/2-inch lengths	2 cups broccoli flowerets, cut into 1-inch pieces
1 large red bell pepper, seeded, cut into 1/2-inch-thick strips	1 cup cauliflower flowerets, cut into 1-inch pieces
1 large carrot, scraped, sliced thin	1/2 cup chopped scallions
	1/2 cup chicken broth
	3 Tbs. soy sauce
	2 Tbs. dry sherry

1. Heat the peanut oil and sesame oil in a large heavy skillet over high heat. Add the celery, bell pepper, and carrot. Stir-fry 3 minutes.

2. Add the garlic, broccoli, and cauliflower. Stir-fry 3 minutes. Add the scallions, chicken broth, soy sauce, and sherry. Cover and simmer 3 minutes or just until the vegetables are crisp-tender. Serve immediately.

Rice with Tomato Flavor SERVES 6

2 Tbs. butter	1 cup water
1/4 cup chopped shallots	1/2 cup canned chicken broth
1 cup rice	Dash of Tabasco
1 medium tomato, peeled, seeded, chopped	Pinch of dried thyme
	1/2 bay leaf

PREHEAT THE OVEN TO 400°.

1. Heat the butter in an enameled saucepan. Sauté the shallots until soft. Add the rice, stirring until the grains are coated with butter.

2. Add the tomato, water, chicken broth, Tabasco, thyme, and bay leaf. Bring to a boil. Cover and bake in a preheated 400° oven for 18 minutes. Remove the bay leaf, fluff with a fork, and serve hot.

Chocolate Oranges   SERVES 6

**4   medium navel oranges, at   Rich chocolate sauce
        room temperature   (pp. 81-82)**

    1. Peel and section the oranges. Carefully remove the membranes. Dry well with paper towels.

    2. Make chocolate sauce following the recipe on p. 51 (chocolate pears). Using a fork, swirl the orange sections in the chocolate to cover. Proceed as for chocolate pears.

MORE VEGETABLES AND SALADS

This chapter is a collection of vegetable dishes and salads that didn't quite fit into the menu format but are so good I didn't want to omit them.

You may serve any of the salads either as an appetizer or as a separate course following the entrée. There are several vegetable dishes here substantial enough to stand on their own. Use them as the basis for creating your own menus or serve them with your favorite meat or poultry recipes.

Puree Blanc   SERVES 6

An interesting way to prepare winter root vegetables. Serve with roast chicken, turkey, or glazed ham.

3 Tbs. butter	4 cups chicken stock (p. 207)
2 medium onions, chopped	or 2 cups canned chicken
2 medium potatoes, peeled	broth and 2 cups water
and sliced	3 Tbs. heavy cream
1 turnip, peeled and cubed	Pinch of nutmeg
1 large celery root, peeled and	Freshly ground black pepper
sliced	to taste
1 small bulb fennel, sliced	2 Tbs. chopped parsley or
	chives

1. Heat 2 tablespoons of butter in a large saucepan over medium heat. Sauté the onion until soft. Add the remaining vegetables and chicken stock. Bring to a boil. Reduce the heat and simmer, covered, for 25 minutes or until the vegetables are tender.

2. Drain the vegetables (reserve the stock for use in soups) and puree them in a food processor with the heavy cream. Season with nutmeg and fresh pepper.

3. Return the puree to the saucepan with the remaining tablespoon of butter and heat through. Sprinkle with parsley or chives and serve in a warmed vegetable dish.

Mushrooms Stuffed
with Prosciutto and Cheese   SERVES 4

12 large mushrooms
2   Tbs. olive oil
1   clove garlic, minced
¼   cup chopped parsley
⅓   cup fresh bread crumbs
¼   cup grated mozzarella
    cheese

3   Tbs. freshly grated Romano
    cheese
1   tsp. dried oregano
2   slices prosciutto, minced
2   Tbs. melted butter

PREHEAT THE OVEN TO 375°.

1. Wipe the mushrooms clean. Remove and chop the stems.

2. Heat the olive oil in a heavy skillet. Add the garlic and mushroom stems. Stir over medium heat until the stems are lightly browned. Remove to a bowl. Let cool. Stir in the remaining ingredients except the melted butter. Mix well.

3. Stuff the reserved mushroom caps with the ham and cheese mixture, mounding it. Arrange the stuffed mushrooms in a baking dish and dribble on the melted butter. Bake in a preheated 375° oven for 20 minutes. Serve hot.

Stewed Red Cabbage with Apples   SERVES 4 – 6

This is a robust dish that's good with pork, duck, and goose.

1   medium red cabbage, 2½–3
    pounds, trimmed and cored
    Salt
¼   cup vegetable oil
1   medium onion, sliced thin
1   Tbs. sugar
3   Tbs. cider vinegar

1   large tart apple (Granny
    Smith), peeled, cored, and
    sliced
½   cup beef stock (p. 208) or
    ½ cup canned beef broth
    Freshly ground black pepper
    to taste

1. Quarter the cabbage and cut it into ¼-inch-thick slices. Sprinkle with salt and let stand 20 minutes. Squeeze out excess moisture.

2. Heat the oil in a large heavy saucepan over medium heat. Sauté the

onion until wilted. Stir in the sugar and vinegar. Add the cabbage, apple, stock, and pepper. Cover and simmer over very low heat for two hours. Stir occasionally and add a tablespoon or two of beef stock or water if the cooking liquid is evaporating. Serve hot.

Potatoes Dauphine   SERVES 6 – 8

In this classic French recipe, *pâte à choux* brings sophistication to the mundane mashed potato.

1	large baking potato		Salt and freshly ground black pepper to taste
1	egg yolk		
1	Tbs. heavy cream	2½	cups vegetable oil
1	Tbs. butter	1	cup warm pâte à choux (p. 204), made without sugar

1. Cook the potato in boiling water to cover for 45 minutes. Drain and peel.

2. Purée the potato with the egg yolk, heavy cream, and butter in a food processor. Season with salt and pepper. You should have 1 cup.

3. Combine the cup of potato puree with the *pâte à choux*. Mix well. Fill a pastry bag fitted with a large round tube with the mixture. Heat the oil in a 10-inch skillet, and when it is very hot, pipe 1-inch-long puffs directly into the skillet. Deep fry until the puffs are golden brown. Let drain on paper toweling. Serve hot.

Potatoes Anna   SERVES 6

Sliced potatoes are carefully arranged in a frying pan, then baked. When done, the potatoes are turned out of the pan onto a platter and you've got a beautifully browned potato cake. This works best when made in a black iron skillet.

3   pounds potatoes
4   to 5 Tbs. butter
Salt

PREHEAT THE OVEN TO 425°.

1. Peel and cut the potatoes into thin slices of even size.

2. Melt 1 tablespoon of the butter over low heat in a heavy 7½-inch iron skillet. Arrange an overlapping layer of potatoes over the bottom of the skillet. Dot with butter and sprinkle with salt. Repeat with another layer of potatoes, salt, and butter. Arrange a layer of overlapping potatoes around the sides of the pan, then add the remaining potatoes, in layers, to the bottom of the pan. Dot each layer with butter and sprinkle with salt. Shake the pan from time to time to prevent sticking.

3. Butter the top layer and press the potatoes down hard with a large spatula. Cover the pan with a close-fitting lid. Bake in a preheated 425° oven for 25 minutes. Remove the lid; press the potatoes down again with a spatula. Bake, uncovered, 20 minutes more or until the top is browned. Remove from the oven. Carefully drain excess butter from the pan, holding the potatoes in place with the lid or a spatula.

4. Unmold the potatoes. Run a spatula around the sides of the pan, place a serving plate over the pan, and quickly reverse the two. Serve the potato cake hot. If desired, garnish the plate with a sprig of parsley.

Sautéed Chestnuts   SERVES 4

Fresh chestnuts taste so good, it's a shame they're such a pain in the neck to shell. Try this when you're not pressed for time.

1   pound chestnuts   **Salt and freshly ground black**
3   Tbs. butter   **pepper to taste**
2   Tbs. minced shallots

PREHEAT THE OVEN TO 450°.

1. With a sharp-pointed knife make a small slash on the rounded side of each chestnut. Place them on a jelly-roll pan with ½ cup water and bake in a preheated 450° oven for 15 minutes or until the shells start to open. Shell

the chestnuts while they are still warm.

2. Simmer the shelled chestnuts in water to cover for 40 minutes or until tender. Drain and pat dry.

3. Heat the butter in a heavy skillet. Sauté the shallots until soft. Add the chestnuts and stir over medium heat until browned. Season with salt and pepper. Serve hot.

Zucchini and Tomato Gratin SERVES 6

This dish is made with panade—a smooth paste of milk-soaked bread. Serve the gratin as a first course or with roasted or grilled meats; or for lunch, with a tossed salad and glass of wine.

1/3	cup olive oil	2	eggs, lightly beaten
1	medium onion, chopped	1/2	cup grated Swiss cheese or a
1	clove garlic, minced		mixture of freshly grated
2	pounds zucchini, sliced thin		Parmesan cheese and Swiss
1	pound tomatoes, peeled,		cheese
	seeded, and chopped	1/2	tsp. dried thyme
2	slices French bread (1/2 inch		Salt and freshly ground black
	thick), crust removed		pepper to taste
1/2	cup milk	1	Tbs. olive oil

PREHEAT THE OVEN TO 350°.

1. Heat the oil in a large heavy skillet over medium heat. Sauté the onion until soft. Stir in the garlic and cook for a minute without letting it brown. Add the zucchini and tomatoes and cook the mixture, uncovered, for 30 minutes or until the vegetables are very soft. Raise the heat to high and reduce the cooking juices.

2. In a bowl let the bread soak in a half cup of milk for a few minutes. Mash with a fork until the panade is very smooth. Stir in the eggs and grated cheese. Season with thyme, salt and pepper. Combine this mixture with the cooked vegetables. Mix well.

3. Turn the gratin into a buttered baking dish (or gratin dish) and dribble 1 tablespoon olive oil over the top. Bake in a preheated 350° oven for 1 hour. The top should be nicely browned. Serve hot.

SALADS

Corn Salad with Tarragon Dressing   SERVES 4

4	to 6 ears fresh corn	¼	cup olive oil
12	cherry tomatoes, halved	¼	cup vegetable oil
1	medium red bell pepper, seeded and diced	½	tsp. Dijon mustard
1	medium green bell pepper, seeded and diced	1	Tbs. fresh chopped tarragon or 1 tsp. dried
2	Tbs. tarragon vinegar		Sald and freshly ground black pepper to taste

1. Shuck the corn and cook the ears in boiling water to cover for 8 minutes. Drain. Let cool. Remove the kernels from the cob with a sharp knife. You should have 2 cups.

2. Combine the corn kernels, cherry tomatoes, and diced peppers in a salad bowl. Whisk together the vinegar, oils, and mustard. Stir in the tarragon, salt and pepper. Pour the dressing over the salad and chill for one hour to blend flavors.

Orange and Onion Salad   SERVES 4

1	small head chicory, torn into bite-sized pieces	1	medium red onion, sliced paper thin
3	small oranges or 3 tangerines, peeled, seeded, and sectioned	2	tsp. sherry vinegar
		¼	cup peanut oil
		¼	cup olive oil

1. Combine the chicory, oranges, and onion in a salad bowl.

2. Whisk together the vinegar and oils. Pour the dressing over the salad just before serving.

Lentil Salad   SERVES 4 – 6

2	cups dried (presoaked) lentils	½	tsp. dried thyme
1	quart water	1	bay leaf
1	medium onion stuck with 1 clove		Vinaigrette dressing (p. 206) made without Dijon mustard
1	large clove garlic, peeled	½	cup scallions, chopped
1	carrot, scraped and halved	½	cup minced onions
1	celery rib, halved	¼	cup minced parsley

1. Put the lentils into a large saucepan with the water, onion, garlic, carrot, celery, thyme, and bay leaf. Bring to a boil. Cover and simmer 30 minutes. The lentils should be tender, not mushy.

2. Drain the lentils and remove the vegetables and bay leaf. Toss the warm lentils with vinaigrette dressing. Stir in the scallions, minced onions, and parsley. Refrigerate. Serve chilled or at room temperature.

Avocado Whip   Makes about 3 cups

2	ripe avocados	3	Tbs. mayonnaise (p. 205)
2	Tbs. lemon juice	3	Tbs. heavy cream
¼	cup olive oil		Salt and pepper to taste

Peel and slice the avocados. Sprinkle with lemon juice. Purée the avocados with olive oil in a food processor or blender. Transfer the mixture to a bowl and stir in the mayonnaise and heavy cream. Season with salt and pepper. This is good with fresh cold shrimp or spooned into hollowed-out tomato halves. Or serve it in individual portions on crisp lettuce.

Greek Salad   SERVES 4

Feta cheese is the "Greek" in a "Greek" salad. This pretty, substantial salad makes a good first course or light lunch entrée.

1	small head romaine lettuce, torn into bite-sized pieces	½	pound feta cheese, cubed
3	ripe tomatoes, cut into wedges	16	Greek olives, pitted
1	small red onion, sliced thin	¼	cup chopped scallions
		½	cup vinaigrette dressing (p. 206)

Combine all the ingredients except the vinaigrette in a large salad bowl. Chill. Just before serving toss the salad with vinaigrette dressing.

Red Cole Slaw   SERVES 6 – 8

1	head red cabbage, core removed	1	Tbs. heavy cream
2	large carrots, scraped and grated	1	Tbs. lemon juice
1	cup mayonnaise (p. 205)		Salt and freshly ground black pepper to taste

1. Cut the cabbage into small chunks and chop it coarsely in a food processor fitted with the chopping blade. Remove to a bowl. Add the grated carrots.

2. In a mixing bowl combine the mayonnaise, cream, lemon juice, and salt and pepper. Fold the dressing into the chopped cabbage. Stir to blend. Adjust the seasoning, adding more lemon juice, salt, or pepper if liked. Chill.

Spinach-Avocado Dressing   MAKES ABOUT 1½ CUPS

½	pound fresh spinach, stems removed, rinsed and dried well	½	cup vegetable oil
2	Tbs. cider vinegar	¼	cup olive oil
2	cloves garlic, peeled		Pinch cayenne pepper
½	small avocado, peeled	¼	tsp. dried cumin
½	bunch parsley, trimmed	½	tsp. dried basil

199

Place the spinach, vinegar, garlic, avocado, and parsley in the container of a food processor fitted with the metal blade. Process until the mixture is reduced to a thin puree (this takes about 3 minutes). With the machine running, slowly add the oils. Stop processing and stir in the cayenne pepper, cumin, and basil. Chill the dressing for 1 hour to develop flavor. Good with iceberg salad (see below).

Iceberg Salad   SERVES 4 – 6

1	small head iceberg lettuce, torn into bite-sized pieces	1	medium cucumber, peeled, seeded, and sliced
1	carrot, scraped and sliced	1	small red onion, sliced

Combine all the vegetables in a large salad bowl and toss with ½ cup spinach-avocado dressing.

Bean Sprout Salad
with Snow Peas and Mushrooms   SERVES 4

½	pound snow peas, trimmed	1	Tbs. lemon juice
¾	pound bean sprouts, rinsed and dried well	2	Tbs. soy sauce
		2	Tbs. peanut oil
¼	pound mushrooms, sliced thin	1	Tbs. oriental sesame oil
		1	tsp. minced fresh ginger

1. Blanch the snow peas in boiling water for 20 seconds. Drain immediately under cold running water. Pat dry.
2. Combine the snow peas, bean sprouts, and mushrooms in a salad bowl.
3. In a small bowl whisk together the lemon juice, soy sauce, and oils. Stir in the minced ginger. Just before serving, toss the salad with the dressing.

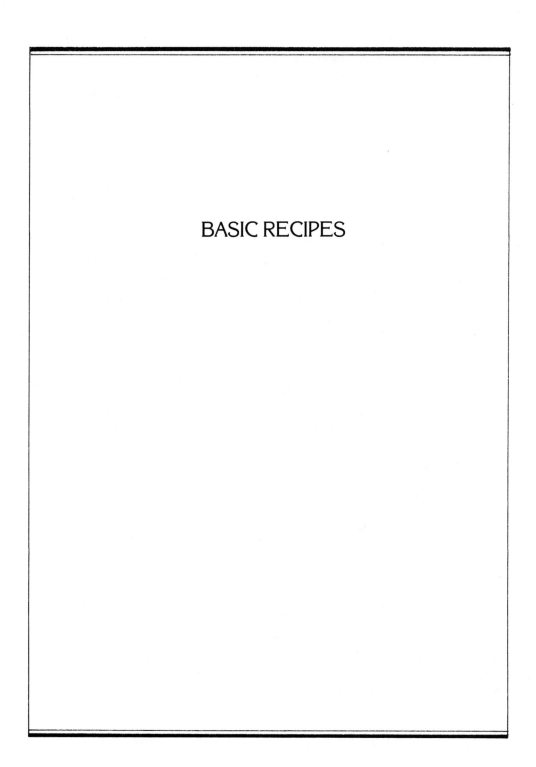

BASIC RECIPES

Pâte Brisée (basic tart crust)

Makes one 8- or 9-inch tart shell

This formula for *pâte brisée* produces a very tender, flaky, buttery crust. It rolls out easily, can be refrigerated for three days, and freezes well for up to a month (defrost in the fridge overnight before using).

1¼	cups all-purpose flour	4	ounces butter (1 stick), softened to room temperature
1	tsp. salt	2	Tbs. cold water

Mix the flour and salt together in a large bowl. Add the butter in small pieces. Using a pastry blender or two knives, blend the flour and butter until the mixture resembles coarse cornmeal. Sprinkle the water over the mixture and continue to blend just until the dough begins to come together—do not overblend. The dough should be pliable, but not damp and sticky. Gather it into a slightly flattened ball, dust with flour, and place in plastic wrap. Let the dough "rest" in the refrigerator for at least 4 hours or overnight before rolling it out. The dough can be made in a food processor fitted with the metal blade. Put the flour, salt, and softened butter in the work bowl and process very briefly, about 15 seconds (here you must be extremely careful not to overwork the dough). Stop the machine, sprinkle on the cold water, and process 15 seconds more. Gather dough into a ball, dust with flour, wrap in plastic, and refrigerate 4 hours or overnight.

FOR A FULLY BAKED TART SHELL:

Select the pan size called for in the recipe. Use either a pie pan or tart tin with a removable ring. Roll out the dough on a clean, well-floured surface to a thickness of ⅛ inch, drape it over the rolling pin, and fit it securely into the pan. Trim off excess dough with the rolling pin. Chill the pastry shell for at least 2 hours. Before baking, prick the bottom of the shell all over with a fork, line the pastry with foil or baking parchment, and fill it with rice, dried beans, or metal pie weights (to prevent the dough from shrinking and buckling while baking). Bake in a preheated 425° oven for 20 minutes. Remove the rice and foil; bake another 20 minutes or until the pastry is golden. Allow the shell to cool on a wire rack. The shell is now ready to be filled.

FOR A PARTIALLY BAKED TART SHELL:

Prepare the tart shell as above. Bake in a preheated 425° oven for 15 minutes. Carefully remove the rice and foil; bake 10 minutes longer. Allow the tart shell to cool; add the filling. Tart and filling are now ready for further baking.

Pâte Brisée Sucrée
(sweet pastry for dessert shells and fruit tarts)

Prepare the dough as in the preceding recipe, substituting 1 tablespoon sugar for the salt.

Crêpes   Makes 12 – 14 crêpes

These paper-thin lacelike pancakes are indeed a wonderful invention. Accommodating themselves easily to a vast number of savory fillings, they can be served for breakfast, lunch, as an hors d'oeuvre, for dinner, or dessert.

Once crêpes are made, they'll stay moist for several hours covered with a dampened cloth, or if you prefer, make them a day or two ahead and refrigerate, tightly covered. Crêpes freeze well and are good to have on hand when guests arrive unexpectedly. To thaw, place foil-wrapped crêpes in a preheated 300° oven for 10 minutes.

¾ cup all-purpose flour	¾ cup milk
2 eggs	1 Tbs. melted butter or
1 egg yolk	vegetable oil

1. Combine all the ingredients in a blender or food processor. Blend for 20 seconds or until the batter is completely smooth. Let the batter rest, covered, at room temperature for 2 hours.
2. Brush the bottom and sides of a 6- or 7-inch crêpe pan with oil. When the pan is almost smoking, pour in a scant ¼ cup batter. Rotate the pan as you pour so that the batter covers the entire surface.

3. When the edges are lightly browned, carefully lift the crêpe with a flexible spatula and turn it to cook briefly on the other side. Remove to a dish. Continue making crêpes until all the batter is used.

Pâte à Choux

(cream puff pastry)   Makes approximately 24 dessert puffs

Fully baked, unfilled puffs freeze very well for up to a month. When you want an attractive dessert in a hurry, simply thaw the frozen puffs in a 400° oven for 5 minutes. They are then ready to be filled with flavored whipped cream or ice cream.

4	ounces butter (1 stick), cut into pieces	1	cup all-purpose flour
1	cup water	5	large eggs
¼	tsp. salt		Egg wash (1 egg lightly beaten with 1 tsp. water)
½	tsp. sugar		

PREHEAT THE OVEN TO 400°.

1. Put the butter, water, salt, and sugar in a heavy 2-quart saucepan. Bring to a boil; be sure the butter has melted completely. Reduce the heat to moderate and add the flour all at once. Beat with a wooden spoon until the mixture forms a mass and comes away from the sides of the pan.

2. Let the mixture cool slightly. Make a well in the center. Using a wooden spoon, beat in the first egg thoroughly. Continue with the remaining eggs, one at a time, making sure each egg is completely incorporated before adding the next. If you have an electric mixer with a flat beater, use it, running at slow to medium speed. The final paste should be smooth and soft.

3. Form dessert puffs while the paste is still warm. Line a baking sheet with parchment paper. Drop the *choux* paste by tablespoonfuls onto the baking sheet or pipe the mixture through a pastry bag fitted with a ¾-inch round tube. Space the puffs about 2 inches apart. Brush the tops lightly with egg wash and bake in a preheated 400° oven for 35 minutes.

4. Remove from the oven; let the puffs cool slightly. Cut them in half and remove any damp dough from their centers. Allow the puffs to cool completely before filling and reforming. Unfilled puffs may be frozen.

Mayonnaise   Makes 1 cup

If you've been brought up on store-bought mayonnaise, fresh mayonnaise will be a taste revelation. Chances are, you already have the necessary ingredients on hand—mayonnaise is nothing more than a sauce of egg yolks, oil, and a bit of seasoning.

You can quickly produce a very thick pale yellow mayonnaise in a food processor. If you prefer a thinner sauce, use a medium-sized bowl and an electric hand-held mixer; whichever you use, remember these two important points: (1) have all ingredients at room temperature and (2) to prevent curdling, add oil to egg yolks very slowly in a thin stream or by drops.

2	egg yolks	¾	cup vegetable oil
1	tsp. Dijon mustard	1	Tbs. lemon juice
	Pinch of salt and pepper	1	Tbs. red wine vinegar

In a small bowl whisk together the egg yolks, mustard, and salt and pepper. Transfer the mixture to the work bowl of a food processor. With the machine running, add the oil in a slow steady stream. When half the oil has been added, stop the machine and thin out the mayonnaise with lemon juice and vinegar. Turn the food processor on again and add the remaining oil slowly. Taste for seasoning, adding more salt, pepper, or lemon juice if necessary. Mayonnaise may be stored in the refrigerator, tightly covered, for up to two weeks.

Hollandaise Sauce   Makes approximately 1 cup

Like mayonnaise, hollandaise is an egg yolk sauce. It is thickened with hot butter rather than oil and is served tepid. Good over asparagus, broccoli, and broiled fish.

4	ounces (one stick) butter	2	Tbs. lemon juice
3	egg yolks, at room temperature		Salt and pepper to taste

1. Melt the butter in a small heavy saucepan over medium heat until it begins to foam.

2. Put the egg yolks and lemon juice, salt and pepper into the container of a blender or food processor. With the machine running, pour in the hot butter in a slow steady stream until it has been completely incorporated into the egg yolks and forms a smooth, thick sauce. Hollandaise should be served tepid; you may keep it an hour over warm water.

Basic Vinaigrette Dressing   Makes over ½ cup

2	Tbs. red or white wine vinegar	½	tsp. Dijon mustard Salt and freshly ground black pepper to taste
¼	cup vegetable oil		
¼	cup olive oil		

Combine all the ingredients in a small bowl. Whisk until blended. Refrigerate.

Currant Glaze   Makes ½ cup

½ cup red currant jelly   1 Tbs. water or kirsch

Combine the currant jelly and water or kirsch in a small saucepan. Bring just to the boil. Use while warm.

Apricot Glaze   Makes ½ cup

½ cup apricot preserve   1 Tbs. water or kirsch

Combine the apricot preserve and water or kirsch in a small saucepan. Bring just to the boil. Strain. Use while warm.

Homemade stocks. We don't always have the time to prepare large quantities of homemade soup stocks, but fresh chicken stock and beef stock should be part of a good cook's repertoire. Nothing improves the flavor of soup like your own stock.

Chicken Stock   Makes 2½ to 3 quarts

4	pounds chicken (this can be a collection of wings, backs, necks, or a 4-pound chicken, cut up)	3	onions, peeled and quartered
		½	cup dry white wine
		1	large clove garlic, crushed
		½	tsp. dried thyme
4	quarts cold water	1	bay leaf
2	large carrots, scraped and halved	3	parsley sprigs
		1	tsp. salt
2	ribs celery, cut in half	½	tsp. pepper
½	cup chopped celery leaves		

1. Combine all the ingredients in a large stock pot or kettle. Bring to a boil. Skim off any scum. Lower the heat and simmer, partially covered, for 1½ hours.

2. Strain the stock. Reserve the cooked chicken for another use. Cool the stock and remove the fat. The stock may be frozen for up to 6 weeks or stored in the refrigerator for a week if boiled every other day.

Note: If necessary, to concentrate flavor, reduce the stock over high heat.

Beef Stock   Makes 2½ to 3 quarts

2	pounds beef brisket, cubed	2	cloves garlic, unpeeled
2	pounds beef bones, cut up	½	cup dry white wine
1	veal knuckle	½	tsp. dried thyme
2	large carrots, scraped and halved	1	bay leaf
		3	parsley sprigs
2	ribs celery, cut in half	1	tsp. salt
2	onions, peeled and quartered	½	tsp. pepper
4	quarts water		

PREHEAT THE OVEN TO 450°.

1. Place the beef, bones, knuckle, carrots, celery, and onions in a roasting pan. Roast in a preheated 450° oven for half an hour, or until the beef is well browned. Remove the vegetables, meat, and bones to a large stock pot or kettle. Pour off the fat in the roasting pan.

2. Pour 1 cup water into the roasting pan; stir and scrape up the brown bits clinging to the bottom and sides of the pan. Add to the stock pot along with the remaining ingredients. Bring to a boil. Skim off any scum. Lower the heat and simmer, partially covered, for 4 to 6 hours. Strain the stock, cool, and remove the fat. The stock may be frozen for up to 6 weeks or stored in the refrigerator for a week if boiled every other day.

Note: If necessary, to concentrate flavor, reduce the stock over high heat.

TIPS, TECHNIQUES, INGREDIENTS

Listed below are suggestions for handling some of the vegetables often used in this book. Also included are a few words about ingredients and techniques that I think you'll find useful.

EGGPLANT is very watery. Salting sliced or cubed eggplant and allowing it to drain in a colander will rid it of excess moisture and ensure the crispness of fried or sautéed eggplant. This technique is sometimes used with cucumber and squash.

TOMATOES frequently require peeling. To do this quickly and neatly, drop tomatoes into rapidly boiling water to cover for 30 seconds. Drain under cold running water. The skins will slip off easily. This technique may be used for onions and peaches, too.

CANNED CHICKEN BROTH AND CANNED BEEF BROTH are perfectly acceptable substitutes for homemade stocks (and great time savers, too). They do tend to be strongly flavored and salty; therefore, in many cases I've suggested diluting canned broth with water. You will probably find that a soup made with canned broth needs little or no additional salt.

SALT as a seasoning for food is largely a matter of personal taste. I use very little when cooking. For most of these recipes I do not indicate a specific amount of salt to be used, but rather the advice "salt to taste."

WHIPPED CREAM should always be made with well-chilled, fresh heavy cream. Do not use ultra-pasteurized heavy cream; its chemical preservatives make it almost impossible to whip. Whip cream in a chilled bowl using either a chilled whisk or chilled blades of an electric beater.

BUTTER is always unsalted in these recipes. This reflects my desire to keep salt intake to a minimum. I think you'll agree that most foods, baked goods and desserts in particular, taste better when unsalted butter is used.

If cooked *SPINACH* is to be combined with other ingredients (eggs, cheese) or pureed, be sure to remove as much moisture from it as possible. Drain in a sieve or colander, then place spinach in a clean kitchen towel and wring it out.

INDEX

218